OPEN-ENDED STORIES

Globe Book Company, Inc.

Englewood Cliffs, New Jersey

OPEN-ENDED STORIES

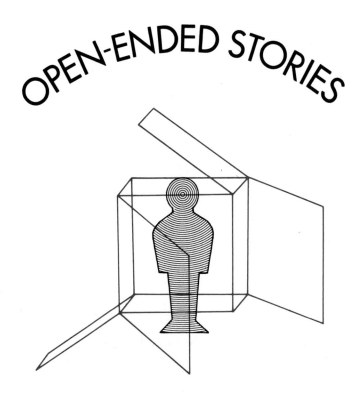

Milton Velder
Edwin Cohen

Edited by Louis Spitalnick and Tom Maksym

Illustrated by Ned Glattauer and Oscar Liebman

PRINTED IN THE UNITED STATES OF AMERICA.
15   16   17   18   19   20

ABOUT THE AUTHORS

Milton Velder received his Master's degree from the University of Maryland. He has taught secondary English in the Baltimore City Public Schools, where he served as English department chairman, and Specialist in English. Mr. Velder has conducted workshops in literary criticism, linguistics and reading simulation. A member of the editorial board of the Maryland English Journal, Mr. Velder is the co-author of Globe's *Journeys in English.*

Edwin Cohen received his Master's degree in education from Johns Hopkins University. In his long and varied teaching career, Mr. Cohen has been a demonstration teacher, and Principal in the Baltimore City Public School system. He has conducted workshops on micro-teaching, questioning techniques, critical reading skills and simulation games.

During the last four years, Mr. Velder and Mr. Cohen have worked on the college level with urban education programs. At present, both are Associate Professors of Education at Towson State College in Baltimore County and are working with student teachers.

CONTENTS

Thematic Key / x
About This Book / xii

1   Mind Your Own Business / 1

2   Run, Baby, Run / 8

3   But I Didn't Know / 15

4   Not Like Jeff / 23

5   Wendy / 26

6 Once Upon A Time / 30

7 Letters To A Soldier / 35

8 He Is Not Dead / 45

9 Let George Do It / 52

10 Willie Lawson For President / 59

11 The Man With The Cigar / 64

12 Walk Proud, Be Proud / 74

13 Play The Game / 80

14 What Now, Sis? / 85

15 Out To Win / 92

16   My Sister, The $3.00 Bill / 97

17   A World Of Her Own / 101

18   Just Like Your Sister / 106

19   My Son, The Doctor / 114

20   Honor Thy Father And Thy Mother / 118

Closing Up The Open Ends: Thinking About
The Stories And Their Endings / 126

THEMATIC KEY

	Page
Mind Your Own Business	1
Run, Baby, Run	8
But I Didn't Know	15
Not Like Jeff	23
Wendy	26
Once Upon A Time	30
Letters To A Soldier	35
He Is Not Dead	45
Let George Do It	52
Willie Lawson For President	59
The Man With The Cigar	64
Walk Proud, Be Proud	74
Play The Game	80
What Now, Sis?	85
Out To Win	92
My Sister, The $3.00 Bill	97
A World Of Her Own	101
Just Like Your Sister	106
My Son, The Doctor	114
Honor Thy Father And Thy Mother	118

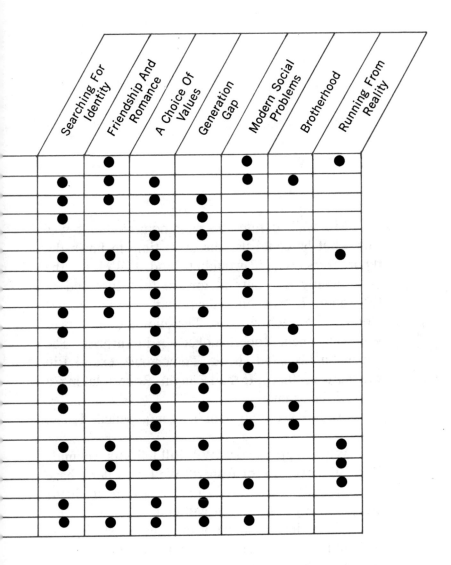

ABOUT THIS BOOK

Bill walked into the classroom. Sure, it was early—but he could use the extra time to finish the report. Mrs. Schmid wouldn't mind. Bill closed the door quietly and hurried toward the other end of the room. It was only then that he saw Robert alone at the teacher's desk. The middle desk drawer was wide open. Robert looked up in surprise. The papers in his hand shook. Tomorrow's exam! Bill was sure of that. He had caught Robert taking a copy of the exam.

"Bill, I was only looking for a pencil. I . . . I . . ."

What happens now? Will Bill tell Mrs. Schmid? Will Bill cover up for Robert? Well, you don't have to wait until next week to find out. *You* finish the story the way *you* think it will end.

This is just a sample of the types of stories you will find in this book. Each situation presented is one that has really happened to someone—and could very well happen to you. Each story is about young people like you. Each story is a little piece of life.

Why are the stories unfinished? They are *open-ended* so that *you* can complete them. They give you a chance to use your imagination and creativity. There is no one right ending to any story. If you have good reasons for making a decision, your ending is as good as any other one.

You will have an opportunity to complete the stories in a variety of ways. You will also have a chance to gain additional skills in the areas of reading and writing. Finishing the stories can be amusing, interesting and rewarding. Life itself presents many situations in which you must make decisions. And so, *Open-Ended Stories* might be helpful to you in solving some of your own problems.

Not all of the endings you supply will satisfy everyone in your class. But in a very real sense you become an author facing the challenge of bringing a story to a fitting conclusion. Remember: there are no right or wrong endings. You are the final judge as well as the creator.

MIND YOUR OWN BUSINESS

Bill was puzzled. That was the second time today Stan had walked by without saying hello. "Did I do anything wrong?" he kept asking himself.

He was even beginning to worry a little. After all, the young men had been buddies since first grade. Now they were in high school. They had been through a lot together.

The bell snapped Bill from his thoughts. He hurried along. Stan would be in his next class. Maybe if Bill cornered him at the close of the period he would explain his strange behavior.

When Bill reached his desk the class had already begun. He looked over at Stan. Suddenly he was startled to find that his friend's eyes were hidden behind a pair of dark glasses. Now Bill couldn't take his eyes off him.

Stan usually helped to make social studies discussion come alive. Today he slumped in his chair, completely tuned out. From time to time, his cheek would twitch. Just before the bell rang, Bill was amazed to see his friend lay his head on his desk. His cheek was twitching more than ever.

But by the time Bill reached the classroom door, Stan had already vanished down the hall. That afternoon, for the first time, Stan didn't show up for basketball practice.

Bill decided to telephone him that evening. He didn't often do that. It was always so hard to talk to Stan's mother. This time their conversation was briefer than usual.

"Can I talk to Stan, please?"

"He's not home."

"When do you think he'll be back?"

"I have no idea," she said sharply and hung up.

The next day, Stan suddenly appeared, his face beaming.

"How you been, Sport?"

"O.K., I guess." Bill didn't really know what to say.

"Sorry I missed practice yesterday," Stan said. "Believe me, I couldn't help it." Stan seemed almost to be pleading.

Bill was feeling more and more uneasy. Then he noticed that Stan no longer wore sunglasses.

"Anything wrong with your eyes?" Bill asked. "They look watery and . . ."

But Stan quickly interrupted him. "Could you let me have a few dollars until next week?" Bill reached into his pocket. This was the second loan in the last month.

Stan took the money, flashed another big smile and walked off. "See you at practice this afternoon," he said.

"How things have changed!" thought Bill. In all the years of their friendship it was almost an unwritten agreement that they would never borrow money from each other.

But at basketball practice that afternoon, Stan seemed his old self. Only during warm-up did Bill notice that Stan's famous timing was off. He was the star of the team, but today he handled the ball hesitantly. He missed five practice shots in a row.

"Can't get them all!" Stan joked. But Bill knew he was upset.

"Anyway, I bet I can still beat you at Indian wrestling," Stan challenged. Bill accepted, secretly hoping Stan still could.

They wandered over to the coach's table. Getting into position for Indian wrestling, elbows on the table, they grasped each other's hand. At that moment, Bill felt a chill as cold, perspiring fingers clamped over his own. Stan's hand was trembling.

"Ready?" Stan asked. They began straining to pin down each other's arm. Usually the young men were well matched. Today it seemed as if all Stan's power had left him.

"Just got me off guard, Sport," Stan quickly said. "I'll beat you this time." Once more they grasped each other's hand. Stan's seemed even colder now. Bill won again without much effort.

"You're getting stronger, Sport, but you won't beat Old Powerhouse again!" For the third time,

they got into wrestling position. Then suddenly Bill understood.

He had caught sight of something on Stan's arm. Hoping he had been mistaken, he looked again. But there it was. The friends' eyes met. Without a word exchanged between them, the secret was out.

Just then the coach blew the whistle to continue practice. As Stan ran off to the middle of the court, his last look seemed to say, "Forget it, Sport. There's nothing you can do."

Deeply shaken by the sight of those pinholes in Stan's arm, Bill stood in a daze as his friend grabbed a ball and tried a few more shots. None connected with the basket. The coach's yell brought Bill back to earth and onto the court.

He fumbled his way through practice, watching his friend out of the corner of his eye. Afterwards, Stan managed to duck out of the locker room without speaking to Bill.

That evening was the most troubled of Bill's life. He couldn't eat; he couldn't sit still. His mother asked him what was wrong, but he couldn't tell her, especially after what had happened to his cousin Fred.

Bill hadn't thought about Fred for a long time. Stan always reminded Bill of Fred. Both were good athletes, both had been school leaders.

Fred had a great future ahead of him, everyone had said. But that was before he had started fooling around with the *stuff*. Bill was still haunted by the memory of the night the police had come. They reported that Fred had been killed while trying to rob a gas station. Poor Fred. How hooked he must have been to do something as desperate as that!

Bill's mother had said at the time, "Someone should have called the police while there was still time to do something. He needed help!" Now, recalling those words, Bill winced. Could he turn in his best friend?

Though his heart wasn't in it, Bill decided to go to basketball practice the next day. The big game was coming up. Bill couldn't let the team down.

Once there, Bill noticed that Stan was missing. But Stan needed help badly. Bill decided then and there to find him. He left his teammates standing on the court.

He didn't have to search too far. Stan was in the

5

dressing room going through the lockers, frantically pocketing money, watches, rings—anything.

"No, Stan, stop!" Bill shrieked, beside himself.

Stan spun around. He was wearing sunglasses again. His hands were shaking badly and sweat was rolling down his face.

"Here," Bill reached for his wallet, "I have ten dollars. Put those things back."

Stan's voice was full of despair. "That just isn't enough."

"Remember what happened to Fred," Bill pleaded.

"Yeah, I know. But that won't happen to me!"

Stan made a move to go, but Bill was determined to stop him.

"You better let me by, Sport," Stan said in a trembling voice.

Bill stood his ground. Stan's fist connected with Bill's stomach. Bill sagged to the floor.

As he came to, jumbled phrases floated through his mind. "Sorry, Sport . . . didn't mean . . . to hit so hard . . . you don't know . . . what it's like . . ."

Bill stumbled along the halls of the school, not knowing where he was going, tears streaming down his face. He hadn't cried like that—since Fred had been killed.

"SOMEONE SHOULD HAVE CALLED THE POLICE WHILE THERE WAS STILL TIME TO DO SOMETHING. HE NEEDED HELP!" Again his mother's words echoed through his mind.

But how could you do that to a friend?

Suddenly Bill saw a phone booth at the end of the hall. All he had to do was dial and say, "My friend is . . . is . . . a dope addict!"

The phone booth seemed to grow larger and larger. Bill stood still for a moment. Then . . .

RUN, BABY, RUN

"It's not every day you get invited to a fancy restaurant, baby," Harris said to himself as he made his way along the crowded sidewalk. For him this was going to be one beautiful day. He stopped for a moment to admire the reflection of his new suit in a store window. "Not bad at all." It was the first he'd ever bought with his own money.

But why was he walking here today? It had been more than five years since he'd passed through the ghetto. But here he was, bumping against people and looking around. Same old buildings about to fall apart. Same old trash in the streets. Same old smells of stale food. Nothing had changed, and Harris almost felt he missed it. He had had some good times in the ghetto and he still felt drawn to it.

But could it ever get him back? Those filthy

hallways. All those poor people crowded together in those rotting tenements. The sad old folks sitting out on their stoops just staring. Why, there wasn't even enough room in the streets to move around.

And the kids! Harris could tell which of them were already headed for trouble. He had spent enough of his life in the streets and in a reform school to know all the signs.

The sights and the memories were now beginning to get to him. He didn't want to feel low, especially today. And what if he ran into someone he knew? What would he have to say after all those years? He began walking faster. Without realizing it, he was almost running. He just had to get away from all this . . .

Before he knew it, he was passing through clean, quiet streets. There were trees planted along the curbs, and even the air smelled cleaner. The ghetto was far behind him, and soon his depressed feelings left him. He slowed down.

But he still arrived at the restaurant much too soon. Jim wouldn't be there for another half-hour at least. To pass the time, he watched the people as they entered the restaurant. He was relieved to see a few black faces among them. Harris still wasn't completely at ease in the white world. "Baby, you'd probably be more sure of yourself washing the dishes in there," he laughed to himself. As a matter of fact, he had worked as a dishwasher several times in the last few years. But he didn't regret it one bit.

"Whew, just look at those prices!" he said to himself, inspecting the menu in the window. But then Jim wouldn't celebrate this day in any other way. Nothing but the best for a good friend on a special occasion.

Jim was such a great guy. Harris wondered what his life would have been like without him. He hadn't especially liked Jim at first. Harris had thought he was just another reform school counselor who didn't know the score.

But he soon found out that Jim was different. Maybe it was because Jim had also come up the hard way and understood what Harris had gone through, and what he still had to do.

Many times Jim had told Harris, "You know, baby, it's up to you."

"Don't hand me that. There ain't no place out there for me. All they have to do is look at me. They've got their minds made up already."

"Listen, baby," Jim insisted, "give yourself a chance. Think as much of yourself as you want others to think of you."

Talks like that had pulled Harris through. Now he knew he'd done the right thing. He'd had enough of reform schools.

Two years before, when Harris had been released, Jim had taken time off to help him find a good place to live. "To make sure you get a new start," he had said, "we've got to keep you out of the ghetto." For Harris it had been strange, at first, living in a neighborhood where the faces weren't all black. He had gotten used to it, though, and he hardly ever thought about the old streets and the old ways. And when he sometimes felt he couldn't make it, Jim was always there to turn to.

They'd been hard years in other ways too. Low-paying jobs with long hours—dishwasher, busboy, porter. All so that he could get a high school diploma. But on the day he walked up to the platform to receive it, Jim had also been there. Harris couldn't have felt prouder.

And now Jim would be there to help him celebrate this biggest day of all. Had Harris ever imagined the time would come when he'd be graduating from a police academy?

He was never quite sure why he had made the decision to become a policeman. Sometimes he thought it was a way of getting back onto those streets—where the kids were. He knew the ghetto and he had paid its price. Maybe he could help keep some of those kids up there from paying it too. Maybe he could be to them what Jim had been to him.

Just then, Harris's thoughts were sharply interrupted by a shrill cry, "Help! Thief! My purse!" He turned just in time to see a black girl snatch away an elderly white woman's purse. Then the girl flew past him, pursued by the woman. Immedi-

ately, Harris took after them. The woman was rapidly running out of breath and he passed her. But the girl was something else. Man, could she run! But Harris finally caught up to her. He grabbed her arm. But she shook him off. Still, he kept after her. At last, he had her!

"Let me go! Let me go!" she screamed and sobbed at the same time. He clutched her tightly by the arms and held her against a car.

Harris looked at her. There was a desperate, dull look in her eyes. He knew that look from the past. She was on something . . .

She began to struggle. He held her tighter. "Why you doing this?" she wept. A group of people were slowly gathering around them. Harris noticed a few black faces among them. And then he realized like a shot that they must have been part of the *gang*. He knew what they were up to. It was called "Working Main Street." And he had taken part in it many times himself.

He looked at the girl's hands. Sure enough, she didn't have the purse. After all, you don't get caught holding the evidence. Harris could have kicked himself for missing that trick. He knew it well enough. He had been sent to reform school the last time for not being fast enough on a job just like this. The girl had tossed the purse to someone in the gang while she was running. He had handed it to someone else, and so forth, until someone got it who could walk away unnoticed.

"What's going on here?" said a policeman as he edged towards them through the crowd.

"Everything under control. Patrolman Brown,

here . . ." Harris was about to say. But another voice broke in.

"My purse! My purse!" Harris recognized the woman's voice. She too was pushing her way through the crowd. "Where is she . . . There she is . . . She took it . . . That *nigger* . . ."

THAT NIGGER! That was all Harris had to hear. It was as if she'd spat in his face. "That nigger, that nigger." Enraged, he kept repeating it to himself. "People like her don't deserve to be helped. Why am *I* doing it?" Suddenly, he dropped the girl's arms and let himself be swallowed up in the crowd.

But for some reason, he didn't make his escape. He stood to the side, watching, listening. There was a lot of confusion. Everybody told his own version of the story. Shortly, they'd have to let the girl go. There was no case against her without evidence and without a witness. Harris was the only witness.

But then he heard that woman's voice again, higher than all the others. "And then some colored man . . ."

"COLORED MAN! Me!" To Harris that was almost worse than *nigger.*

"Calm down, lady," he heard the policeman say. "Can you identify the man who caught the girl?"

There was silence as the white woman looked from black face to black face. For a second, her eyes stopped as she looked at Harris. Then she turned to the policeman and said, "No, I just can't tell. They all look alike . . ."

For Harris that was the last straw. "Her and her stupid white mind. *They all look alike!* Why she's no better than the girl who stole her purse. Worse!" He turned away in fury.

But in that instant, Harris suddenly found himself face to face with—Jim! On the other side of the crowd. It was him all right. But how long had he been there? Had he seen the whole thing?

Of course he had. Harris could tell. And he had understood the whole thing. Now Harris looked Jim straight in the eye. Would Jim give him some hint about what to do?

But Jim's expression said only one thing. "Baby, I can't help you out on this one. It's up to you . . ."

Harris took a step toward the crowd. He was not really sure of what he was doing. He looked from the shrieking white woman to the sobbing black girl. All he had to do now was walk away . . . or turn to the policeman. Suddenly, he made up his mind. He . . .

BUT I DIDN'T KNOW

Marge was in one of her moods again. "Nothing to do . . . same old stuff." The angrier she got, the faster she pedaled. Each turning of the wheels cried out, "I'm bored! I'm bored! I *must* get away! I *must* get away!" Without realizing it, she turned her bike into Hillside Park.

There were many things Marge wanted to forget. School!—a real bore . . . useless junk . . . a bunch of teachers who couldn't care less about her. Friends!—a real joke. Empty talk . . . same faces . . . same everything. And guys!—all with one thing on their minds. And Larry wasn't any different.

The hill was getting steep. Marge struggled along, thinking about things at home. She didn't care for her father. He just sat glued to the television set and only stopped for another beer. "Shut up!

Can't you see I'm busy?" was the only conversation he made with her. As for her mother, she almost didn't exist. About all she ever had to say was, "Sorry, Marge, there's too much work to be done. We'll talk later." Later never came.

"At last." Marge gave a sigh of relief. The top of the hill. A chance to be alone and forget for a while. Marge's Hilltop. No one else allowed.

She leaned the bike against the tree and climbed onto a large rock. Marge's Throne. There, she loved to look down at the houses and think that people below didn't know she was watching them.

Suddenly she had a strange feeling that she wasn't alone. At first, she was afraid. Then she became a little curious.

Slowly, cautiously, she looked around. Someone else *was* here. Worst of all, a guy! He had no right to be on her private hilltop!

But the young man didn't even seem to realize she was there. He was reading. Something called "Civilization." "Who would want to read that stuff!" she thought. "Ugh!"

Marge stretched out near the rock. The sun felt good on her face. It was the first real spring day. The hill seemed so beautiful that she nearly forgot her problems. The buds in the trees had just begun to bloom, splashing yellows and reds and purples against every possible shade of green. Marge suddenly wished she knew what kind of trees they were. Why hadn't she learned *that* in science class instead of having to label those silly carrots?

The silence was broken by music. She looked around. It couldn't be! The young man had a tran-

sistor radio. And he was listening to *that* kind of music—the stuff Mrs. Able, the music teacher, said the class ought to appreciate. Marge almost laughed out loud—only squares listen to that kind of music!

Then she noticed that the young man had picked up something. It was a bird, though she hadn't been sure at first. At that moment he looked up and found her watching him. He gave a quick smile. Marge turned away. But curiosity got the better of her.

She walked over. He looked up and smiled again. Then he turned his attention to the bird. "Its leg is broken. It must have fallen from the tree," he said, gravely.

Marge watched him make a splint of twigs for the bird's leg and carefully wrap a piece of his handkerchief around it. Then he gently stroked its head and said, "You'll be all right soon." He put the bird down in the grass, and he and Marge watched as it hopped around as best it could. "It's horrible to be lame," he said.

And then suddenly remembering himself, he laughed and said, "Oh, I'm sorry. My name is Pete."

"I'm Marge." She hesitated a few moments. "Can I tell you something?"

"Sure."

"You know, I was very angry when I first saw you here. I come here a lot and I'm almost always alone. I think of it as my own private place."

Pete's face expressed worry. "Oh, I didn't mean anything personal," said Marge. "I just didn't want anyone around. But I'm glad you're here," she added quickly, "really I am."

The hill was quiet. Pete's smile returned. The bird was still hopping around. "How did you know how to fix the bird's leg?" Marge broke the silence.

"I know a little about birds. My hobby is training pigeons."

"Oh!" Marge was surprised. She had never known anyone interested in training pigeons. "What do you do with them?"

He told her about training birds: "I feel an excitement each time I see the birds take off, free for a while, flying where they want." Marge listened closely, because of the way he explained it, because he made her feel a part of what he was saying.

"You must like nature a lot," Marge said. "I wish I knew more about nature. I was looking at the trees before and realized how little I knew about them. See how smart I am!"

Pete began to name the trees and tell her some things about them, but suddenly he stopped. "There I go again. I must be boring you."

"Oh, no, please go on, Pete," Marge said. She really meant it. She had never really seen trees the way Pete was helping her to see them today.

Marge had never thought the afternoon would turn out so enjoyable. Even the music pleased her. "What are they playing?" she asked.

"One of my favorites. Beethoven's Ninth Symphony," he answered. "Did you know that Beethoven was completely deaf when he wrote that music? It's amazing how someone can overcome a handicap. Maybe our bird will have a chance to survive."

"Pete, you know, you're amazing. I don't think I've ever known anybody who was interested in so many things. I bet you never get bored."

Pete smiled, "Sometimes you have to get interested in things. Otherwise you have too much time to feel sorry for yourself."

"I'll bet you're not a basketball fan," Marge said, thinking how much Larry and her father were interested in sports.

"I can't *play* basketball," Pete said, lowering his eyes, "but I'm a great spectator."

There was silence between them for a few moments.

"Marge," he said, finally, "I think *you* are an amazing person. You're one of the few people I've really been able to talk to. I'm pretty much of a loner. That's why I've had to learn so many things."

19

Marge suddenly understood. No wonder she felt so comfortable with Pete even though she had just met him. She, too, was a loner, though she hadn't admitted it to herself before. Pete had helped her really see herself for the first time.

Marge laughed. They both laughed. It was the kind of laughing that said they shared a secret about each other. Something like this would never happen with Larry.

Then Marge realized it was late. "It's 5:30. I have to be going."

"I'm sorry. Will I be able to see you again?" asked Pete.

Marge made a quick decision. "Pete, the rec center is having a dance Saturday night. My boyfriend Larry is tied up with a basketball awards dinner. Could I ask you to go with me?"

"Gee, that would be great, but I'd be no fun at a dance."

A look of disappointment came over Marge's face. But Pete continued, "What if I got tickets for the rock concert at the stadium for Sunday night?"

"Pete, I'd love it."

"Suppose I call you at 6:30 and tell you the details."

He handed Marge a pencil and paper. While she was writing her address and telephone number, Marge saw a big man get out of a car and walk toward them with a warm smile.

"It's my father," Pete said. "He's come to pick me up." He introduced them.

And then it happened. Pete's father leaned forward and lifted Pete up from the ground. Then the big man supported him slowly to the car. Marge's eyes widened when she saw the brace on Pete's left leg dragging across the grass.

Pete leaned out of the car window to remind her about calling her at 6:30. Then the car was gone. Marge sat down, tears streaming down her cheeks.

Then she became angry with herself. Why hadn't she understood some of the things he was saying . . . the lame bird . . . the composer who overcame his handicap . . . the dance . . . basketball. Pete hadn't tried to hide anything. The brace seemed so large and ugly as he had limped away.

She realized that he had talked about himself that way because he thought she understood. How could she have been so blind? Then she realized! She had made a date with a . . . a cripple. What would the others say when they saw her with him Sunday? And what about Larry? Every eye would be on her as she and Pete entered, his left leg dragging in that brace. All of those whispers, and the noise of the brace against the floor.

Marge was so dazed that she didn't realize that she had pedaled the long way home. It was after 6:30 when she got there.

Even her mother was concerned. "Marge, where have you been? Your dinner is cold. By the way," she added, "there was a call for you about ten minutes ago. Some young man. But he said he'd call back again."

Just then the telephone rang. Marge's heart seemed to miss a beat. It rang again. Then she heard her mother say, "Marge . . . just a minute . . . Marge! Telephone for you."

Marge picked up the receiver and heard Pete say, "Hi, Marge! It's all set for Sunday. My father will pick you up at 7:30. O.K.?"

Marge swallowed hard—then said, "Pete . . ."

NOT LIKE JEFF

Stevie's angry again. After school he usually comes into the kitchen for milk and cookies. Today he just storms into the house and runs upstairs without even saying hello. What a moody boy! Who knows what's bothering him this time! I'll just ignore him. He'll cool off. Then maybe he'll come downstairs and tell me what it's all about.

It's funny how different Jeff is from Stevie. I'm their mother, but sometimes I find it hard to believe they're brothers. Jeff seems so much older, though they're only two years apart.

But then Jeff always makes a better impression. "A real movie star," Aunt Lil calls him. "Our own little football pro," Uncle Benjie says. A fine boy. Friendly. Outgoing. The whole family agrees.

Now Stevie—when there's company, he's up

in his room drawing. And if he comes downstairs, he just looks at magazines while everybody is talking. Aunt Lil asks him how he's doing in school and he shrugs and says, "O.K." Uncle Benjie asks him if he saw the Lion-Colt game and of course he says no. Stevie's not interested in sports. He doesn't even like to watch T.V. He doesn't like anything other kids like.

It's Jeff who does the talking. Baseball. Football. Basketball. He knows every team, every score, all the averages. He plays on two varsity teams himself and he could be on others, but he just doesn't have enough time.

After all, he's class president and president of the school debating club. And if that weren't enough, he's pulling an A average and still manages to earn extra spending money. His father and I allow him to work part-time at the drugstore. We'd prefer he didn't, but he's such a capable boy . . .

Stevie struggles along in school. Not even a B average. His teachers can't understand why. During her last conference with us, Stevie's science teacher, Mrs. Jones, asked him why he didn't work as hard as his brother Jeff. Do you know, that boy just picked himself up in the middle of what she was saying and walked out of the room. I made him apologize to her the next day.

But that's the sort of thing he does. Funny things bother him. He sticks to himself, and he draws. That seems to be the only thing he really seems to care about. It's the only subject in school where he gets A's.

His art teacher even sent us a note telling us

we ought to encourage him. Oh, we try. But how can you get excited over a drawing of a bowl of apples? Jeff always tells Stevie that he likes his pictures. Jeff is such a kind boy.

Well, other people like Stevie's drawings too. One of his pictures is in a display of school art at the department store. It isn't a bad picture at all. We all went to see it the first day it was hanging— the same day we celebrated Jeff's big debating club victory. What a debate that was! I've never been so proud of him!

But it's that department store that's also caused all this bother. It's giving a dinner honoring those students whose work is on display. We were even sent special invitations. But wouldn't you know, Jeff's playing in *the* big game in Carsonville tonight. I told Stevie last night that we can't go to both. My husband feels one of us should go to the game and the other to the dinner. Of course, we'd rather go to the game. I wonder if Stevie would be all that hurt if we didn't go to that dinner.

Oh my! He's coming downstairs now. What should I tell him?

WENDY

If you don't want to hear my side of this story, you can just close your book—if your teacher will let you. But then you'll never know why I feel Wendy's wrong—and why Wendy feels she's right.

Wendy's in high school, and she's really just like any other kid her age. At least that's what I think, and I ought to know. I'm her father. Well, you be the judge.

Wendy's got a sister named Karen. She goes to a college that's just fifteen minutes from home. But I spend $500 extra every year so that she can live in a dorm. You see, we want her to have a good social life . . .

But I'm only telling you this to show how much we care about our kids. Wendy doesn't have anything to complain about, either. We live in a beautiful house in the suburbs and she gets more spending money than most girls her age do.

Still, Wendy has always been a problem. Ever since she started school, her teachers have been telling us how bright she is. That's just great. But then we'd get notes from them that began: "I would like to have a conference with you."

Then we'd hear that Wendy wasn't doing quite as well as we thought. "It's really not her work," they'd say. "It's her attitude . . ." Maybe Wendy is too bright for her own good.

So I asked Wendy, "What's the problem?"

"Oh, it's those dumb teachers," she'd answer. "They just don't know what they're teaching."

Now you figure that out. These people go to college for four years, and then this kid says they don't know anything! But that's not all she had to say.

"And they always ask us to do dumb things. They make us read textbooks that don't mean anything to us. And when we ask them, 'Why can't we talk about *important* things for a change?' they just tell us we don't know what's important. Or they say we have to stick to our program of study."

She likes only one teacher. Her social studies teacher. But I know that man. He's a real weirdo. They should fire him. Wendy probably gets all her crazy ideas from him.

But that's beside the point. Wendy isn't really old enough to decide what she should be learning in school. When I was her age, I never questioned what the teachers did or said. I went to school to

learn. But most kids today go to school to fool around. It's like a social club for them.

If it was up to her, Wendy would just "rap" all day about politics or ecology—all kinds of things she doesn't really know anything about. Thank goodness there are a few students left who aren't that way.

Excuse me a minute. I'll be back. Wendy just came in . . .

Well, this is the last straw! Wendy just got home from school with a note for me to sign. I have to give her permission to . . . You won't believe this. Her nutty social studies teacher is working on some project called "Modern Problems" or something like that. And he wants these school kids to organize—a protest march!

Right! A protest march! They're supposed to demonstrate in front of some factory downtown that's been polluting the air. Then they've made arrangements to speak to two state senators. These kids! Did you ever hear anything like it? They think they're going to change the world overnight.

High school kids should have other things on their minds and leave the protesting to us adults.

But what really shocks me is that the school is actually encouraging them. It ought to know better. A school's business is to teach American history and science and math, not to get its students involved in foolishness.

Wendy will probably be out there in front. I find it harder and harder to reason with that girl.

Well, do you see now what's wrong with Wendy? I have a feeling that most of you are not like her. How about taking some time to think about her problem. Then maybe you can write me and tell me how you feel about it.

Maybe you'll want to start your letter this way: Dear Mr. Gilmore,

I have read about Wendy, and I . . .

ONCE UPON
A TIME

"Once upon a time. . . ." Does every story that begins that way have a happy ending? Once upon a time . . . there lived a pretty girl named Mary Calvos . . .

She was popular—very popular. Was there ever a weekend when she didn't have to turn down several young men asking for dates?

Mary's schoolwork didn't suffer, though. She went out only on weekends, and she was smart enough to get by without too much effort. But sometimes her parents worried. Mary thought that they watched too much T.V. and read too many magazines. She was sure that they worried too much about the younger generation and all of the "terrible" things they did.

They weren't really old-fashioned. But what parents don't live a little in the past? "When I was your age . . ." Every now and then, Mary's father would begin one of his lectures with those words. Mary would smile politely until he had finished. She didn't have to listen very carefully. She had heard it many times before. But sometimes she got the feeling that her father worried too much about her.

Mary's mother showed a bit more trust in her. "Dear," she would say, "your father and I know you would never do anything wrong . . ."

She was right. Mary loved her parents. And deep down, she understood that they gave her so much freedom because they both counted on her to do the right thing. But then, once upon a time, something happened to Mary Calvos. It started innocently enough—a simple date—a movie, something to eat and then home. She liked the boy right away. She could see he was a warm, understanding person.

They began to go everywhere together—to football games, to rock concerts. Even going to a movie and having a hot dog with him seemed a special experience.

None of the others she had dated were like him. He was so beautifully sensitive and aware of so many things. When they were out together, he made her see things differently. A simple flower became a whole garden as he described its petals, its shape, its color. A piece of music became a whole symphony as he helped her sense every note. The whole world became a new and beautiful planet as she saw it through his eyes, through his feelings, through his sensitive explanations. He made her feel important.

But then, once upon a time, something happened to Mary Calvos. It had been a great evening. The rock group had been wild. If it's possible to get high on music, they both were as high as could be. "Let's just sit and talk," he said as they parked the car near Wood's Farm.

They *did* talk, but somehow he sounded a little different that night. His talk was kind of disorganized, more way out than she had ever heard before. She should have guessed what was going to happen next.

He reached into his shirt pocket and pulled out a cigarette. That wasn't unusual. He smoked too much; Mary had told him so many times. But this time wasn't like the others. She quickly guessed that this cigarette was no ordinary one. He lit up and inhaled deeply. "Wow!" he said after he had slowly exhaled the smoke.

"Take a puff," he said, offering Mary the joint. "You haven't lived until you've tried one of these."

"No! Take me home." There was anger in her voice.

For the rest of that night Mary couldn't stop thinking about it. "He uses that stuff. Why him of all people? Why does he have to do it? He's the kind of person who shouldn't need it at all."

He called her on the phone the next day. It was good to hear his voice again. But what could she say to him? She knew she would never see him again as long as . . .

He kept calling—once, twice a day. He tried to explain. "But, Mary . . . it makes this world more bearable . . . it hides all the ugliness . . . I can't face life without it."

But Mary didn't understand. She told him again and again that she wouldn't see him until . . . "I'll help you," she said.

"I'll try, Mary, I'll try . . . You'll have to help me."

Mary tried. But she knew that something was different. He was very quiet. It was hard to get him to talk at all. His voice seemed to show that he was on edge and uptight. Somehow he wasn't the same person she had fallen in love with.

Two weeks passed. It was Saturday night . . . movie night. As soon as Mary opened the door to let him in her house, *she knew*. She looked at his eyes and realized that she had lost her battle.

They walked to the car without saying a word to each other. As they were driving, he was the first to break the silence. "I guess it's time to have another talk. The movie's not that important."

Mary nodded her head in agreement, afraid she would cry if she tried to speak.

They drove to Wood's Farm in silence. He parked the car and immediately began to talk. "Mary, I tried . . . you don't know how much . . . I couldn't make it . . . I'm back on it now . . . I'm a new person since . . ."

"But . . ." she interrupted him. She tried to reassure him . . . to make him understand . . . one slip didn't mean that . . .

"You're wrong, Mary, I need to see the world in my own way. I guess I'm looking for my "Once-Upon-a-Time Land" with purple mountains and gentle giant-like trees that keep on worshipping the sun . . . and this is the only way I can find it."

He took out a joint, lit it slowly, and inhaled deeply several times. "Look . . . there . . ." he paused several minutes, "it's my polka-dotted bird in my candy-striped tree!"

Mary looked, but she didn't want to see *his* world through his Once-Upon-a-Time eyes.

"And, Mary," he continued in a low voice, "I can't take my trip to that world alone. I need someone to share it with."

Mary understood perfectly what he was saying and what he wanted her to do. She loved him deeply. She knew that it was all over unless . . .

She watched him inhale. He passed the joint to her. She hesitated, then took it and . . .

LETTERS TO
A SOLDIER

January 20

Dear Bob,

I know girls back home are supposed to write cheerful letters, but we're all so worried. You left three weeks ago for the war zone and you haven't written once. Your mother says she is going to call

Washington if she doesn't hear from you soon. It doesn't help when people say the Defense Department would tell us soon enough if something did happen to you.

Bob, do you realize it was exactly a year ago today that we started going steady? I feel depressed thinking how carefree our lives were then. But these thoughts certainly won't cheer you up. And I'm not helping myself either. My mind is with you, but I have to study if I want to graduate. Please write.

With all my love,
Gloria

January 23

Dear Bob,

That wonderful postman brought me another letter from you today. I already know every word by heart. I almost wept when you wrote how much you missed me, because I long to be with you.

But I'm also glad to hear you're not so lonely and that you've made a good friend in your platoon. Ron seems a lot like my friend Clara, the one who is always organizing peace demonstrations. In fact, Clara got me to attend a meeting of the SWI (Students Who are Involved), and I have already learned things about the war that I never realized before. I hope you approve. Somehow, going there makes me feel closer to you.

But maybe you'd rather my letters weren't so serious. I suppose things are serious enough where you are. Forgive me.

All my love,
Gloria

January 30

Dear Bob,

I wish the world would shrink so that we wouldn't be so many miles apart.

Your last letter described my mood exactly. I also feel alone when I'm with my friends. The things they say and do seem so silly to me now. Because you're over there. And because of Clara too. She's opened my eyes to so many things. I guess I've really begun to change.

That's why I think maybe you shouldn't be so hard on the other men in your platoon. I'm relieved to know you don't drink or turn on like many of them do. But I bet they must be scared to death about seeing action. Anyway, I'm glad you have Ron to talk to when you feel low. Do you think Ron would mind hearing from Clara? They both seem to make the same vibes, and I thought it might be good for both of them.

Deepest love,
Gloria

Dear Bob,

Was feeling frantic, but now I understand why I hadn't heard from you. Your first battle. It must have been horrible for you. But Bob, don't be ashamed of the way you felt and the things you did in action. Being a hero doesn't mean a thing. I don't want you to bring home medals. I love you because you're a sensitive, sympathetic man. I can't imagine that you'd go into battle with hate in your heart.

Clara got a letter from Ron today. She's very worried about him. You know she's not against desertion, but she's afraid he may ruin his life.

SWI called together a special meeting tonight. The school board won't let us use the building any more. It says we've gotten too militant. We have to plan a new course of action.

All my love,
Gloria

————————————

March 1

Dear Bob,

You're right. I'll never be in your shoes. But I do try to understand. You say that drinking is the only way you can make it through each day. But I'm scared for you all the same.

That battle you described was too horrible to

think about. Can the people in your outfit really have enjoyed such slaughter? War seems to bring out the worst in everybody. Well, not everybody. . .

Not even a hundred people showed up for our peace march, and Clara has been suspended for organizing it. We suspect the same thing will happen to other members of the club. I'm grateful to the peace movement. It's taught me more in these last few months about the way things really are than I learned in eleven years of school.

I shouldn't criticize people too much, though. Just a short while ago I thought all peaceniks were kooks. People at home are so uptight. Mom doesn't approve of what I'm doing, but Dad's the real problem. His slogan has become "America, Love It or Leave It." He actually told me he's ashamed of me. He's even more narrow-minded than the principal.

Clara hasn't heard from Ron for some time. I told her what you wrote me about the way he's changed. She's scared that he may go to pieces.

Bob, try not to think about the present. That's how we'll both make it through this nightmare.

> With deepest feeling,
> Gloria

March 3

Dear Bob,

Here's a P.S. to the letter I just mailed. Clara telephoned. She's received a kind of farewell letter

from Ron. He's had it. He's planning to desert.
It's almost as if he were committing suicide.

He confessed to Clara that he's on drugs:
"to help me forget all about the bashed-in skulls
and torn bodies," he said.

Bob, do you think talking to him will make any
difference? I know how desperate he must feel—but
won't he ruin all his future chances in civilian life if
he runs away?

Love,
Gloria

———————

March 15

Dear Bob,

Clara refused to return to school even though
her suspension's been dropped. And she was only
two months away from graduation. Can you blame
her?

Nobody here seems to notice that the world is
falling apart. The big thing on everybody's mind is
the Sweetheart Dance!

And I've been sitting here crying for the last
two hours, and trying to think of things to say to
console you. But I know there is nothing I can say!
What you have seen in action in the last few weeks
would be enough to drive anyone out of his mind.

Don't be ashamed of your tears. You wouldn't be human if you didn't cry.

I love you. Please try to hold on.

Your own,
Gloria

April 7

Dear Bob,

Is Ron really missing in action? Or did he just take off?

Bob, I understand what you're going through, but it hurts so when weeks pass without a word from you. Just a note would do—even a piece of paper with "Hi!" on it.

Things don't look like they can ever be the same again for anyone.

All my love,
Gloria

May 17

Dear Bob,

Nothing from you since the middle of April. It's hard to carry on a one-sided correspondence.

I sleepwalked through graduation. I had to

do it for Mom and Dad. It would have meant the world if you had written.

Clara is forming a commune with some of the other SWI members in one of the poorest neighborhoods in the city. She says that's where the U.S.A. should really be fighting its wars. I wish I could join her—but that would mean giving up college in September, and, worst of all, breaking with my family. I just haven't got the courage to do that!

I guess this also means I'll be seeing less and less of Clara. And it was her friendship that kept me going all this time.

I pray that I'll be hearing something from you soon.

Faithfully,
Gloria

_____

June 1

Dear Bob,

The telegram just said, "Your son was wounded in action." How cruel official notices can be!

I'm going over to your mother's house now to be with her.

Please, I beg you, write! I can't tell you how worried we all have been.

Love,
Gloria

Dear Bob,

What a relief to find out that your leg is healing and that the doctor thinks there will be no lasting injury.

But your leg is no longer the main problem. You, yourself, said, "I'd rather go through life with a damaged leg than a damaged mind." Yes, you have killed other people. But it was the senselessness of war that made you do those things. With the treatment you're getting, I know you will come to stop hating yourself. But the mind takes longer to heal than the body. Have patience.

Bob, there are ways to make amends. We can devote the future to helping other people. That way we can make a better world for ourselves, too.

Hopefully and lovingly,
Gloria

Dear Gloria,

What more can I say? I'm sorry. Sorry I've hurt you with my silence—sorry that we live in such a rotten world.

There's no other way to say it. I can't tell you that I love you. I no longer know what the word *love* means.

I wish I could say to you that I will soon be home and that we can start living again. But I can't. At this point I don't know what the word *living* means any more than I know what *love* means.

Gloria, I can't make it. It's no use trying. Please try to forgive me. I don't think I'll ever be able to make anyone happy again. I'm just no good. Try to understand.

> With all that's left of me,
> Bob

August 19

Dear Bob,

When your letter arrived, I didn't want to open it. I somehow knew what it would say. I . . .

HE IS NOT DEAD

October 7

Dear Diary,

I thought I'd find the same old faces and hear the same old talk at Mike's party. But there was a difference. Eric was there. He's Mike's cousin from Chicago. That Eric really knows how to dress. And by the way, he's just about the best looking boy I've seen in years.

We didn't get to talk much to each other, but he seemed interested. He's more sure of himself than the other boys I know, and he has all kinds of wild opinions about things. Some of what he said made me a little nervous, but I'm definitely attracted. I hope he asks me out.

Dear Diary,

That Eric's so groovy! I grilled Mike about him on the phone last night. I don't think Mike cares for him much. Eric came to the U.S.A. with his family about ten years ago. Mike used to write to him once in a while but he stopped. He said Eric and he had different ideas about everything, but he wouldn't go into detail about it. That Eric grows more mysterious by the moment. How I wish he'd call!

Dear Diary,

We have a date! No words wasted. Right to the point. He reminded me of a Marine sergeant in on old late-night "flick." Wow! Hope I didn't sound too eager. But I had a feeling that I'd better not fool around with him. I can tell he doesn't like to flirt. He upsets me. I hope I'm going to like what I find out about him.

Dear Diary,

First Date! He had already decided what we were going to do. Not a thought about what *I* might want to do. Should I have gotten mad? I guess I like being bossed around a little for a change. He sure makes all the other boys I know seem wishy-washy.

But I must say I didn't dig those stickers on his car. ARISE! HE'S NOT DEAD. They said stuff like that. When I asked him if he was religious, he just laughed. In fact, he made me feel kind of stupid. Anyway, he acted very superior about everything and everyone. Sometimes I think I could easily hate him. But he really is beautiful. There's no doubt about it: I'm definitely intrigued . . .

October 29

Dear Diary,

I've probably watched more World War II movies on the *Late Show* with Eric in the last two weeks than I've watched before in my whole life. He cheers when the Germans invade Poland. He seems to enjoy watching people tortured by the Gestapo. I bet he'd also get a kick out of watching the police whack civil-rights demonstrators or war protestors.

I told him I thought war movies were dumb and brutal, but he doesn't take a word I say seriously because I'm a girl. I know I ought to drop him, but I guess I'm stuck on him. He seems to like me too. He brings me presents and he wants to take me out all the time. I just don't know what to do. He's too weird!

Dear Diary,

Eric took me to his club party to meet all his mysterious friends. I still can't get over what happened. Secret handshakes. Code words. THE MASTER RACE WILL CONQUER and HE IS NOT DEAD tacked up in big letters all over a gloomy basement lit up with candles.

Soon after we got there, Eric and a bunch of the boys disappeared into a back room. I was left alone to talk to all these strange people. I suppose they thought I was as creepy as I found them. I heard one or two of them using uncomplimentary names for people of different races. I thought the whole thing must be some kind of weird joke.

When Eric returned I told him I wanted to go home. At first he didn't want to take me. And when we finally did go, he was really mad. He drove wild and fast, and a policeman stopped us.

It was when Eric opened his glove compartment to find his registration card that the whole thing became absolutely clear. There it was, a black arm band with ⊹ on it. After listening to his friends all evening, I would have been a dope not to figure it out. But I guess I was hiding my head in the sand. I just didn't want to believe such things about Eric.

He knew what I was thinking, too, but it didn't bother him at all. He put the arm band on and began to tease me. He told me I just didn't understand anything serious or important. When I got out of the car, I told him I didn't want to see him any more.

And then I slammed the door shut. I'm sure I heard him laughing. The whole thing was very scary. I won't ever see him again, I swear!

November 23

Dear Diary,

Eric called, and there's no use denying that I'm hooked. I've been so miserable in the last weeks that I almost called *him*. He came over and spent the whole evening explaining his philosophy to me. He says that if the American people had really understood what was going on thirty years ago, they would never have joined the war. He says that's why we're in so much trouble now. And he said things like "Only the Superman can purify America!" He gets so worked up it's almost exciting. But in a way it's almost funny, too. I think he's all wrong, really, but I can never explain myself very well when I'm with him. He won't listen anyway. He's just too sure he's right.

Sometimes I think he likes me enough to change his ideas. Maybe he'll just grow out of them. I have to be patient. I love him so.

December 3

Dear Diary,

There's no point trying to change him. I think he's crazy. He actually believes I've come to agree with him because I don't argue any more.

Actually, I'll be so ashamed if any of my friends spot him on parade next Saturday. My folks will make me stop seeing him for sure if they find out.

The parade wouldn't be so bad if I didn't know it was going to lead to trouble. That club of his is only looking for an excuse to start something. I got such a fright the other day. I found out that Eric keeps a loaded gun under the seat of his car. And he's got a new bumper sticker too: GET RID OF REDS, NOT GUNS! Eric says it looks like there's only one way to cure America, and it's got to start somewhere.

I ought to go to Dad for advice, but Eric would never forgive me if I repeated some of the things he's told me. And Dad will never understand how much I love Eric.

December 8

Dear Diary,

I'm worried to death. All kinds of nasty things are happening around town. Some shopkeepers had their windows smashed with rocks and then some Blacks were beaten up by a gang. And yesterday some public buildings were sprayed with paint.

Eric must be involved in all this, but he won't admit anything. I was in tears last night when we went out. He said I was acting like a little fool . . .

Dear Diary,

It's too horrible! Eric and his friends are about to fire-bomb a bank on Second Street and blame it on war protestors. I overheard them making plans yesterday. But if I tell the police, Eric will be arrested and that will be the end of everything. Maybe I should go to his father. Maybe if I begged him to stop . . . I'm so mixed up. I've got to think things out. But there isn't much time left . . .

Dear Diary,

I . . .

LET GEORGE DO IT

Sometimes I wish I had never met George. Don't get me wrong. George is my best friend. In fact, he's my only friend. But I don't always understand him. Sometimes he does the craziest things. Maybe crazy is the wrong word. *Strange* would be better.

That's why I'm sitting outside the principal's office with him. I haven't said much to him because I really don't know *what* to say. I need time to think. If I talk to George, he'll only confuse me. He always does.

Sometimes I wish I could be more like him. He must have nerves of steel. He's reading a sports magazine. How can he be so calm at a time like this! But that's George.

I guess you're wondering what this is all about. I'll try to explain so that you can understand why I'm so worried and mixed up.

I'll start by telling you about myself. My name is Tom Smith. That's right—Tom Smith. There must be a million people named that. But I guess it's the right name for me because it isn't unusual at all. You see, I've always been the kind of person people don't even seem to know is around.

But maybe it's my own fault. I've never tried to belong—or even wanted to belong. Until I met George I was the guy who always ate lunch alone and then sat by himself in the school yard. Nobody bothered me. But that was O.K. with me.

Even my teachers look at me as if I weren't there. That is, except for Miss Green, my English teacher. She's always called me Thomas—not Tom. But I'll tell you more about her later because Miss Green is part of the problem.

As I was saying, whenever my teachers call on me in class, they either point at me or glance quickly at their seating chart. I guess that's because I never gave them any trouble. I've always done my work and got fair grades. But I've never bothered my teachers, so they've never bothered me.

Things haven't been much different at home. You see, my mother died when I was born, and I've had a lot of different housekeepers taking care of me. Now there's only Dad and me at home. He's O.K. as Dads go. He always gives me everything I ask for, and I get a pretty good allowance. He leaves me alone too. He goes out every night but that's all right with me.

George and his mother moved here from another town about three months ago. His father deserted his mother when George was still small.

George can't even remember what he looked like. George's mother leaves him alone too. He says she has an important job. That's why she's never around.

When George first came to our school, he made a big hit with everyone. He's a good-looking guy, and he has an easy way about him. The gals went wild over him. He was invited to more parties and dances in one week than I'll probably go to in my whole life.

And the guys liked him too. He was a good athlete and everyone wanted him on his team. They loved his jokes. I didn't understand all of them, but I guess I must have been pretty dumb.

You're probably wondering how two such different people became best friends. Well, honestly, I don't understand either. I wouldn't pick me as a best friend . . .

. . . But this is how it happened. One day he walked over to me during lunch. I was sitting by myself as usual, at the end of the table. He just said, "Mind if I sit next to you, Tom?" Man! Was I surprised!

It felt strange talking to someone during lunch. To tell the truth, I didn't really do much talking. I mostly listened. But it was fun just listening to George.

Before long, he started dropping by my house a couple of times a week. He was behind in his school work and needed some help. We really didn't get much done, though. Instead, we watched T.V.

Then George started coming by every morning before school. Usually he would ask to copy my homework. I didn't much like that. I knew it was dishonest. Well, maybe not *so* dishonest. Anyhow, I was afraid that I would lose George's friendship if I didn't give it to him.

I guess I was wrong. Maybe I wouldn't be in this mess if I had said no. You see, it's the homework that really started the trouble. But there I go again, getting ahead of my story.

Before long, George was at my house every night. It was great spending all that time with him. But I also wondered why he didn't seem to be so popular any more. When I asked him about it, he just said, "Who needs that bunch of kids."

We became even closer friends. We went to movies and bowled and went out for pizza. It was fun doing things with someone.

Except I usually ended up paying for everything. George never seemed to have any money. I just don't know what he did with it. He always seemed to be borrowing. But I really didn't mind too much. Anyway, Dad had increased my allowance.

Most of the time being with George was fun. But there were a few things about him that bothered me. Well, maybe more than bothered me. Sometimes I was actually scared. He did things that I was sure would get him into a lot of trouble. Really crazy things.

More than once he took stuff from the five-and-dime store. He just walked out with it. "That's what separates the men from the boys," he said, when I asked him why he had done it. You should have seen all the stolen things he had in his room. . .

But you still don't know why I'm sitting outside the principal's office.

Remember Miss Green, my English teacher? Well, she caught on that George was copying my homework, and did she let us know it! I guess I didn't take her warning too seriously, after all.

I did stop giving George my homework, but when we had to write a composition, George just couldn't do it. He really tried hard. But it was just no good. He really needed help. So I decided to do it for him.

I thought I was smart enough to write the way George did. But I guess Miss Green was smarter than both of us. She knew right away who had done it. And she really blew up. She said she was going to have us suspended.

Man, was I scared! What would my father do when he got the letter from school? "I hope tomorrow never comes," was all I could say to George as we left the room.

"It won't come if we play our cards right," George said.

"But what can we do?"

"We're going to beat Miss Green to the punch," George threatened. "We'll go to the principal's office before she gets there. Will you back me up no matter what I say?"

"Sure, I'll back you up," I replied hesitantly. Anything was better than being suspended, I thought at that moment.

We rushed down to the office and asked to see the principal. "It's very important," George insisted.

The secretary asked us what was so important. "It's very personal," George said.

"There's someone in his office now," she said. "But you can wait if you want to."

. . . So here we sit. Fifteen minutes have passed already. I'm scared. I don't know what George will say. He could say anything. Now the visitor's coming out of the office. A few minutes more and we're with the principal. I'm shaking like a leaf. George has started talking.

You'd never believe what he's saying! Lies about Miss Green—really ugly lies. About the bottle she keeps in her desk drawer. How she sometimes can't walk across the room. George is so convincing that I nearly believe the story myself.

Something in me wants to shout, "No! No! It isn't true! It's all a lie!" But every time I open my mouth nothing comes out.

"When we discovered the bottle in Miss Green's desk drawer, she said she would have us thrown out!" George adds.

There is silence for a few seconds. Then George says, "Tom can tell you too. We both found the bottle."

The principal turns to me. "Is all this true, Tom?"

My heart is pounding. I open my mouth to answer, but nothing comes out. Then I take a deep breath, swallow, and say . . .

WILLIE LAWSON FOR PRESIDENT

Everyone had said no black student could win an election at Grover High. But Willie Lawson had been elected President of the Student Council.

Willie thought he probably owed his victory to his black supporters. But he wasn't really sure. A top student and a fine public speaker, Willie was popular with many white students as well. That's why Willie had decided to run for office. He thought he could be the one person to bring everyone together.

For a while, Willie had really been hopeful. He knew things would not be easy for him. "BLACK STUDENT TO RUN GROVER SCHOOL," ran a local newspaper headline soon after his election. And when a small fight broke out in the school cafeteria, the same paper announced, "RIOT FOLLOWS BLACK STUDENT'S ELECTION." A little fight and they called it a riot! Things like that upset Willie, but he knew that a lot of people were still not ready to change their attitudes.

Willie had expected other problems as well. Sure enough, Grover's Black Power leader, Tyrone Brown, had cornered Willie between periods. "We've got it made, Brother!" He slapped Willie on the back. "Now we get that black students' lounge. And remember, don't let them stick us with hand-me-downs. This school's got enough bread for brand-new furniture."

Willie felt resentful. Had all his black friends voted for him just to be their spokesman? Sure he was black, but he was also Willie Lawson. And as Council President he felt he ought to be responsible to the whole student body. Why couldn't everybody accept that? But Willie knew that before long Tyrone and his crowd would be calling him "Uncle Tom" if he didn't act for them only.

But then, some of Willie's white friends had begun to bother him too. "Willie Lawson," said Allan Cates one day, "you know we voted for you because you're the only one to handle those black militants." He wondered if Allan and his friends had thought he was "Uncle Tom" all along.

Willie was even approached by Eddie Graham. Eddie was a *John Bircher,* and every black student in Grover considered him a racist. Yet he had the nerve to ask Willie to use his influence in getting the school to organize an "America First" celebration. Did people like Eddie figure that a black president was so grateful to be in office that he would be eager to please anyone?

Everyone made demands and everyone gave free advice. Little by little, Willie was getting more and more confused. He had always thought he was "middle-of-the-road." He felt many things were wrong at Grover High. He objected to the way many students' needs were neglected or ignored. But he also knew that these problems could not be solved overnight. In his campaign speech, Willie had stated, "The Student Council President will have to know how to be fair to everyone." Now Willie wondered if it would ever be really possible for him to forget that he was "Willie Lawson, *Black* Student Council President."

Now, a month after his election, a few "Willie Lawson For President" posters still hung in the halls of Grover High School. And Willie stood sad and alone at the door of the auditorium. The second school council meeting was about to begin. And something was up. Willie could feel it in the air. Already, the school auditorium was packed and, more unusual still, there seemed to be about an equal number of black and white students.

Willie was just about to enter when he suddenly felt someone touch his shoulder. "I know you're with us all the way, Brother," Tyrone Brown whispered.

"What's this all about?" Willie demanded, but Tyrone passed quickly ahead of him into the room. Willie took his seat on the platform and called the meeting to order.

But the minutes had hardly been read before Tyrone demanded to be recognized. As he took the floor, he said, "Mr. President. I speak for the black students present here. We are told to stand every day in the classroom while the Pledge of Allegiance is said to the American flag . . ."

"Right on!" a voice shouted.

"But we," Tyrone continued, smiling, "the black students of this school, do not believe that flag stands for us."

"Right on! Right on!" other voices called out.

"We demand that we be allowed the right to pledge our allegiance to our own flag . . . The Black Liberation Flag."

"Hey, just a minute," Allan said as he jumped up. "I object. We're all Americans here. The American flag represents us all . . ."

"Oh yeah?" yelled an angry black voice. "Well it doesn't represent me."

"Then why don't we have the Italians salute the flag of Italy and the Jews pledge allegiance to the flag of Israel while we're at it?" asked Allan in an equally angry voice.

"Order, order!" Willie's voice could hardly be heard above the shouting that had suddenly erupted all over the auditorium.

But Tyrone was not finished. "Mr. President," he said. Everyone suddenly quieted down. They knew that something important was about to happen. "Mr. President, I was saying, you have heard the demands of the black students of this school . . ."

Willie's head was swimming. Could everyone see how unsure he was?

"Willie," Tyrone's voice sounded again, "you're president here. Don't be afraid to let them know whose side you're on. Say something, man . . ."

Willie stood up, closed his eyes, then looked straight and hard at the black and white faces before him. "I . . .

THE MAN WITH THE CIGAR

Paul sat in the waiting room. He was feeling more and more impatient. Every time someone in white passed by, he jumped up from his chair. Dr. Jones had said that the operation would only take an hour, but three hours had already passed and still there was no news.

Paul knew he'd better stop walking back and forth to the water fountain when he wasn't even thirsty. He had to relax. In the condition he was in, he would never be any help to his team in the big game.

Still no sign of Dr. Jones. Paul sat back and looked around the waiting room. Most of the people who had been there earlier had already gone. The only ones left were a boy and his father—and the man with the cigar.

Who was he? When Paul had arrived at the

hospital early that morning, the man was already there, sitting in the same chair. He seemed to move only to flick the ashes off the end of his cigar. Paul didn't know why, but he was beginning to feel annoyed by that man and his cigar.

Paul picked up a magazine, but he couldn't concentrate. Suddenly, he heard a voice. "You're Paul Johnson, aren't you?" Paul looked up. The boy had come over and was standing before him.

"Yeah, I am." Paul smiled—he always enjoyed being recognized. "How do you know my name?"

"Oh, I've seen your picture on the sports page lots of times," the boy answered, "and I watch you play in all the games. My father is taking me this afternoon to see you in the state championship."

"That's great!" Paul liked the boy. "I'll make my first touchdown today just for you."

The boy's face lit up. "Gee!" he said. "Someday I'm going to be on the football team. I want to be as great a star as you are—or like my dad was—Matt Holmes . . ."

"Wow!" said Paul excitedly. "Is your father Matt Holmes?" Everyone had heard of Matt. He was almost a legend. He had been Central High's most famous athlete.

"Yes," said the boy proudly. "And I'm Matt Junior. But everybody calls me 'Chip' because I'm supposed to be a chip off the old block!" Matt smiled from across the room and got up to join them.

Paul enjoyed talking with the great Matt Holmes. The time flew by, and Paul began to feel much less tense. Before long they were talking like old friends. Matt told Paul about his wife's operation. Paul told Matt about his hopes of going to State University the next fall and of someday playing pro football.

Then Paul began to admit how worried he felt about his mother. "I just can't understand why she's been in that operating room so long."

Suddenly, a man in white entered the waiting room. "That's my wife's doctor," Matt said.

Good news! Matt's wife was doing fine. Matt and the boy could go up and see her.

"Well, good-by son," said Matt. "Hope everything goes well with your mother. Hope we'll be seeing you at the game this afternoon, too."

"And don't forget that touchdown you promised me," Chip added.

"I won't," Paul replied, trying to smile. He watched them disappear down the hall. Now he felt alone again. But that man with the cigar was still sitting there. There was a long silence. Suddenly the man smiled at Paul, showing yellow, stained teeth. Paul felt very uncomfortable.

At that very moment, Dr. Jones entered. His expression was grave. Paul could tell that the news wasn't going to be good. "She's doing fine now," the doctor said. "But there were a few problems that we couldn't foresee until we operated."

"Will she be all right?"

"I think so. She'll have to take it easy, though. It'll be some time before she can go back to work. And . . . we're going to have to get a practical nurse to stay with her for a while. It's all going to run into a lot of money, I'm afraid. Is there anyone in your family who can help?"

"No, sir, there isn't." Paul lowered his eyes. "There isn't anyone left on my mother's side, and we haven't seen much of my father's family since he died . . . But the football season will soon be over; then I can get a job right away. I'll just have to put off college for a year . . ." Paul couldn't speak any more. He was afraid his voice would give away his feelings.

"I'm sorry, son," Dr. Jones said understandingly as he shook Paul's hand.

"Can I see Mom now?" asked Paul.

"No, she's still in the recovery room," said Dr. Jones. "I doubt if she'll be out before late evening."

Sad and disappointed, Paul left the waiting room. Soon he was outside on the street, not quite knowing where he was going or why.

Suddenly he looked at his watch. Only two hours before the game, and he hadn't eaten a thing all day. At that moment, Paul smelled something familiar. Sure enough, the man with the cigar was standing a few yards away from him. "Is he following me?" Paul asked himself in amazement.

The man took the cigar out of his mouth. "Hello, Paul," he said. "Sorry to hear about your mother. I wonder if we could have a little talk. Can I buy you some lunch?"

The man was short and fat. He wore glasses so thick that Paul could hardly see his eyes. There was something a little scary about him. "Sorry, I'm in a big hurry," said Paul. "Got to run now." He dashed quickly across the street as the light changed. Then he turned the corner and entered the nearest lunchroom.

Soon after he was seated at the counter, Paul smelled that odor once again. He looked around and found the man with the cigar seated on the stool beside him. "I'll take a cup of black coffee," said the man to the waitress.

"What do you want?" Paul finally asked angrily.

"Calm down, kid. I'm here to help you. I'm a great football fan, you know. And I've been watching your career pretty closely . . ."

There was a pause. The man drew closer to Paul and began to speak in a low voice. "You know, I heard what the doctor told you. What a shame to have to give up your football career, and the way things are going, you may never get to the university."

"What's it to you?" growled Paul.

"Money, right? You need it; I've got it."

Paul was getting angrier by the minute. "You're not offering something for nothing. What's in it for you?"

"Well, son . . . " The waitress brought them their orders, then left. "Well, son . . . there's a little something you could do. It pays well. And if you do it right, there might be even more money . . . especially when you get to State . . ."

"And what exactly do I have to do for you, Mister?"

"Simple," the man replied. "You miss a couple of passes this afternoon. You get paid. Understand?"

Paul couldn't believe his ears. "You're kidding . . ."

"Listen, kid. A cool thousand will buy a lot of medical help."

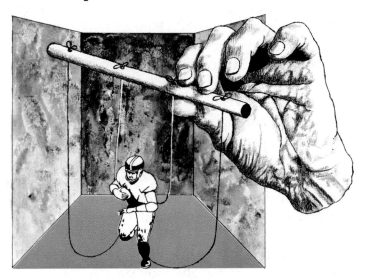

"A thou . . ." Paul had heard that people were always trying to fix ball games, but no one had ever approached him before. He was frightened, but he was also angry. "You know, people like you should be arrested," he said. He took a dollar out of his wallet, slapped it on the counter and left without finishing his lunch.

Paul was upset. He decided to walk all the way to the stadium in hopes that it would help him calm down. When he got to the locker room, most of his teammates were already in uniform. They were sorry to hear about his mother.

Paul got into his uniform and warmed up as much as he could. He did a little running and caught a few passes. But something seemed to be wrong. His timing was off. His muscles just weren't obeying him. He was too tense. His mother . . . that man with the cigar . . . He just had to get all that out of his mind!

The signal came and the team ran out on the field. The crowd cheered. Paul usually loved the cheers, but today he had a feeling that they might not be cheering at the end of the game.

The roar died down. Suddenly Paul heard someone yell, "Yeah, Paul!" Then he saw Chip in the stands, waving wildly. Matt was at his side. Paul felt a little better. He smiled and waved back at them.

Then Paul caught sight of someone else. He was sitting just a couple of rows behind Chip and Matt. Paul could almost smell the smoke of that cigar in his mouth.

The game started. Before long, Paul had the ball and was running. His confidence had returned. Then it happened. The ball just fell out of his hand. The other team got hold of it and scored their first touchdown. They kicked for the extra point and made it. That was only the first of several errors Paul made. At half time, Paul's team was losing, 14–6.

It was quiet in the locker room. For the first

time that season, Central was not leading at half time. Nobody blamed Paul, but he knew he had let his teammates down. Paul sat in a corner by himself. Suddenly he looked up and saw Chip and Matt enter the room. "Don't worry about it, son," Matt said. "I've played worse games than that in my time. And considering how you must feel . . ."

Paul was glad they'd come. He began to relax again. When they left, he called after Chip, "Remember, that first touchdown's for you!"

But on the way to the field, Paul noticed the man with the cigar waving at him. Paul gave him a look that said, "I'm going to win this game in spite of you. You won't upset me any more."

The third quarter was like old times. Paul ran forty yards to score a touchdown. The crowd went wild, and Paul could see Chip jumping up and down, yelling at the top of his voice. Paul waved to him as if to say, "There's your touchdown, Chip."

The extra point was good. At the end of the third quarter, the score was 14–13. Central was clicking. The fourth quarter would tell.

But the fourth quarter was a tough one. With only seconds left in the game, neither side had scored. Paul's team had the ball. Their only hope was to try a long pass. Paul was wide open to receive. Then, out of the corner of his eye, Paul caught sight of the man with the cigar . . . The throw was a good one, but Paul missed. Time ran out. Central lost, 14–13.

Central had lost the game and the state championship as well. Paul felt that he just couldn't face his teammates yet. So he walked out of the stadium and to the park nearby. He took off his jersey and his shoulder pads and he threw himself on the ground. "Why? Why? Why?" he kept asking himself. "Had that man with the cigar really made me lose the game?"

He stayed there a long time. Finally, he thought he'd better get back to the locker room.

When he got there, everyone else was gone. He took off his uniform but decided not to shower. He wanted to get to the hospital as quickly as he could. Paul opened his locker to get his clothes. An envelope fell out of the locker and onto the floor and its contents spilled out. There lay ten one-hundred dollar bills!

Paul just stared at the money. Then he understood. The man with the cigar had thought that Paul had lost the game on purpose.

Paul's first thought was to go to the police and tell them everything. But would they believe him? And what about the scandal that might follow?

Wouldn't people always be suspicious of him after that? And what would it all do to his mother?

But then, for a brief moment, another thought crossed his mind. If he kept the money, all his problems would be solved. No more worries about his mother's medical expenses. No more worries about going to State in the fall. After all, the game was over, and . . . Paul quickly picked up the money and stuffed it in its envelope. He hurried into his clothes. He had to get out. The envelope still in his hand, he approached the locker room exit. There, standing in the doorway, was—the man with the cigar! And for a short man, he looked very large to Paul.

With a steady, determined walk, Paul . . .

WALK PROUD, BE PROUD

The theatre was coming into view. Pat's footsteps began to quicken. Her heart was beating fast. Her first ballet performance! She still couldn't believe it was really happening.

There was still an hour before curtain-time, but she had to get there early to take it all in. Suddenly before her was a large theatre poster. "TODAY—AMERICAN BALLET THEATRE IN SWAN LAKE," it announced. It also showed a beautiful photograph of the dancers in their costumes. Pat could hardly tear herself away. "Someday I'll be on a poster like that," she whispered to herself.

Finally, she walked through the big doors into the lobby of the theatre. She felt as if she were in an enchanted palace. Her feet sank into the deep red carpet. Huge glass lamps hung overhead. And the wide marble staircase seemed to invite her up to share a new world of dreams.

For a moment, Pat felt out of place. There were so many strange faces around her—and most of them were white. They all seemed to be staring at her and wondering, "What is that black girl doing here?" But Pat told herself it was only her imagination. So she quickly joined the line to the ticket window.

As Pat looked around she saw many other young girls. Most of them seemed so happy as they talked with one another. And how well-dressed they all were!

Pat's clothes were clean and presentable. Her mother had made sure of that. But there was no denying that they looked old-fashioned and worn. After all, they were hand-me-downs from the white families Pat's mother worked for in the suburbs. "It's not important what's on you," Pat could still hear her mother saying as she waved good-by to her that morning. "What really counts is what you've got inside. Walk proud, be proud."

In the midst of her thoughts, Pat found herself listening to a voice behind her. "And Mother," said the voice, "could we go shopping later this afternoon? I'll need a new dress for the dance . . ."

"It's just another one of those rich girls from the suburbs," Pat said to herself. But a part of her was praying that no one could see the neat mending job on the hem of her skirt.

". . . And I think I'd better have my ballet lesson changed from Wednesday to Thursday . . ." the girl continued.

Ballet lesson! Pat would have given anything to take a ballet lesson.

"And I won't be home for dinner on Friday, Mother. I had to change my date for tutoring in the city . . ."

"Oh," thought Pat, "one of *those!*" She didn't really know why, but she had always hated "those rich do-gooders." They thought they would change the world by helping some black kids a couple of days a week. Pat just couldn't help turning around to catch a glimpse of her.

The girl was blonde and very pretty. She didn't look like she had a care in the world. Pat decided she hated her, though she wasn't sure just why. Maybe it was because she seemed to have everything Pat ever wanted. Maybe it was because she was white, and seemed so smug . . .

But Pat must have looked at her strangely, or far too long, because the girl suddenly spoke to her. "Hello. My name is Linda Jackson. And this is my mother . . ."

"They must be the kind of people my mother works for," thought Pat. She felt so uncomfortable that she wished she could disappear into the ground.

"Where do you go to school?" Linda asked.

"Dunbar."

"Oh, I thought I recognized you. I tutor there on Mondays. Maybe we can get together some afternoon . . ."

"Phony! Phony!" Pat said to herself. "She talks to me for about three seconds and already she wants to be my friend! And all because I'm *black,* and people are supposed to be nice to black people these days."

"And I also take ballet lessons here in town. Maybe you'd like to come with me one day . . ." Pat thought she saw Linda's mother give her daughter a nudge that was meant to say, *"Take it easy!"*

"Go with her to her ballet lessons!" thought Pat. "Doesn't she know that poor people like me can't do things like that? Shall I tell her how many lunches I did without to save enough money to buy this ticket?"

Pat was glad she was getting close to the ticket window. Soon she'd be able to get away from that chattering Linda and her mother.

"Can I help you?" asked the man behind the window.

In a low voice she answered, "One $2.50 ticket for this afternoon's performance, please."

"Sorry. All we have left are $5.00 and $7.50 tickets."

For a moment, Pat just stood there. "Thank you," she said finally in a voice that was about to break. She was sure she was going to cry, so she

moved away from the window as quickly as she could.

Just then she heard the man call out to her, "Wait a minute! I do happen to have a $2.50 ticket left . . ."

Pat's face lit up into a smile. She reached into her purse and counted out the money. It was all in nickels, dimes, and quarters. When the man handed her the ticket, she felt more pleased than she could say. She'd miss a hundred more lunches to have this feeling again!

But as she walked away, she looked at the ticket. Something was wrong! The ticket said $5.00!

When she returned to the ticket window, Linda and her mother were still there. For an instant, it crossed her mind that she ought to have said good-by to them. But she had been so confused, so happy and yet so unhappy . . .

"Pardon me, sir," she said to the ticket man, "I think you made a mistake. You gave me . . ."

"It's no mistake," he said. And then Pat noticed that he and Linda's mother exchanged a glance. All of a sudden, she realized what had happened. Pat had paid $2.50 for a $5.00 ticket because Linda's mother had somehow motioned to the man that she would pay the extra $2.50.

Pat's heart sank. But she knew what she had to do. "Walk proud, be proud," her mother had told her. "Please return my money," she said to the ticket man with all the courage she had. Then she turned and looked straight into the woman's eyes. "I may be black, but I don't have to accept charity . . ."

With trembling hands she gathered up the money and headed towards the door. She hoped she would be outside before she burst into tears. But she wasn't going to run. She was going to walk out *proud!*

Outside, on the theatre steps, she could feel the sobs shaking her whole body. Tears streamed down her cheeks. Pat sat down and let go.

Just then, she felt someone touch her shoulder. She spun around. There, standing above her, was Linda's mother. There was silence for a moment. Then their eyes met. "Pat, I'm truly sorry," the woman said in a sad voice. "I know I didn't handle that very well . . ."

Pat wiped her tears quickly and stood up. She thought for a moment, and then . . .

PLAY THE GAME

I suppose I ought to be grateful to my Aunt Alma. She always gives my folks and me expensive gifts, like the car she promised me for my next birthday. She also pays for my summer camp, and Dad says she wants to send me to college when I graduate. But I'm beginning to think that we're something like her favorite charity. The worst of it is that she seems to think she can run our lives just because she has a lot of money.

Every year her visits get harder and harder to take. Or maybe I'm getting older and can understand things better. Like this year I could tell in advance she would be more trouble than ever. First of all, I'd never seen Mom so uptight about getting the house tidy for her. It's true that Aunt Alma has a habit of looking into drawers and even under rugs. But this time the house was already cleaner than usual.

And then one morning, Mom looked me over with a strange smile and said, "Bruce, don't you think you could cut your hair this week? And maybe dress a little—differently for a change? You know how your Aunt Alma is."

That was all she said. My folks never insist on things like that. But I was a little hurt and a little mad anyway. They'd never complained about the way I look before.

As far as I was concerned, there was no decision to make. I like my hair the way it is. I brush it every morning and I wash it twice a week. You can't say it's messy just because it's long. And I take a lot of time and trouble choosing my clothes. They're in the latest style, they're comfortable, and I keep them clean. My friends think I'm a great dresser. So why should I have to cut my hair and change my clothes for Aunt Alma just because she's rich?

When Aunt Alma arrived, we really rolled out the old red carpet. And naturally she brought us a batch of expensive gifts, including an album of all nine of Beethoven's symphonies for my "cultural enrichment"—whatever that means.

Mom was right, of course. As soon as Aunt Alma saw me she almost screamed, "Look at that boy! Next thing you know he'll be taking drugs. How can people let their children go around like that?"

The next evening I found five or six boxes of new clothing on my bed. White shirts, dark, baggy pants, lots of ties—things that kids used to wear maybe twenty years ago. None of us could figure out where she got them. She had removed all the labels and tickets so that we wouldn't be able to return them. But that's O.K. I won't wear them anyway.

The next thing to tick me off was what she did to my room. Aunt Alma always stays in my room because it's the biggest and sunniest in the house. One day I looked in and found she'd taken all my stuff down—my wild posters, my gadgets, even my great black light—and thrown it all out! Mom hadn't done a thing to stop her. She said that Aunt Alma thought she was doing it for my own good because "those kinds of things will just lead to drugs!"

I tried extra hard not to explode, but it was bound to happen. Of course Aunt Alma's a snob. She claims her ancestors came over on the *Mayflower,* and everyone knows that she thinks my father married beneath himself. But that's all in the family.

On Saturday my club held its meeting at my house. We're big on ecology, and right now we're working on a recycling project. "Bill who?" or "Frank who?" she asked automatically as I introduced my friends to her. And when she found out, she said, "Oh, you're Italian," or "You must be Irish."

If that wasn't bad enough, when I introduced Marv *Goldberg* to her, she said, "You're JEWISH!" And boy, the *way* she said it! I know Marv. He was pretty upset, but he didn't show it.

I waited till that evening, when I had cooled down a little. Then I let her have it. I had thought the whole thing out. First I told her I respected her

because she was an older person and my aunt, but that I had rights too. I told her my hair and my clothes and my room were personal matters that she ought to respect as much as my own parents did. Finally, I told her she had no reason to pass judgment on my friends because of their race or religion.

You would have thought she had been struck by lightning. She tore out of the place without even bothering to pack her clothes. The last thing she said to me was, "And you can forget about getting that car!"

While she was waiting for a cab my parents tried to patch things up. They told her that young people always have had their own styles and that boys today are more mature and independent than they were a generation or two ago. But she wouldn't hear them out.

Later on, when she had gone, Dad took me

aside and said he thought I should have played along with her. "Look what it can get you," he said, "if you'll just play the game."

So I'm sitting up here in my room trying to think of something to write to Aunt Alma. Mom says it has to be done. Dad leaves things up to me, but I think he more or less expects me to write. Still, I honestly don't understand what they expect me to say. They think it's important for my future that I stay on her good side. Maybe so, maybe not. And they also think it was wrong of her to say and do the things she did . . . but . . .

Well, here goes—
Dear Aunt Alma,
    I'm . . .

WHAT NOW, SIS?

September 14

Dear Sis,

College is going to be great this semester. I got
the courses I wanted, and I even get to sleep late two
days a week. Psychology looks like it's going to be
my favorite subject. The instructor really knows
his stuff, but he can also be a lot of fun. Who knows,
maybe I'll like psychology enough to major in it. It's
still too early to tell though.

I know you're doing great at Morton State, so I
won't bother to ask. You always were the brain of
the family, and I know you'll get as many A's as
you did last year.

Mom writes that everything's about the same at home. But tell me what's been happening to you. How's your social life? I know MSC has a better teaching program than this school, but it's really too bad you couldn't switch up here. Living away from home is great. Nobody to watch your every movement. You're responsible for yourself.

Oh well, got to go. Only ten minutes to get to gym. Write soon.

Love,
Johnny

September 28

Dear Sis,

Glad to hear you're having fun at State. That guy Rob you spoke about sounds interesting. Maybe I'll be going to a wedding soon, huh? (Just kidding!) So he's Jewish. Wow! I wonder what Mom and Dad will have to say about that.

By the way, I'm sure you know Mom held another meeting of the Women's Association to Save the Neighborhood. Does she seriously hope to keep that Italian family out of the neighborhood? But I guess I shouldn't underestimate her. You remember that Polish family last year? And all they wanted to do was open a store.

Mom also told me about Dad's big speech at the "America Is Right" meeting. I bet you're still hearing about it. Gee, sometimes I'm so glad to be far away from all that.

Well, anyway, things are happening to me. I went to visit another fraternity last night. They asked me to pledge, but I just can't decide. Some of the other "frats" look good too. But there are one or two that I wouldn't go near. Some of their ideas—about who "belongs" and who doesn't. Being with them would be just like being at home. Oh well, let them do what they want. To each his own. But they're not for me.

Oh say, I didn't tell you. I'm getting a new roommate today. Louis had some problems at home and couldn't make it back this year. Hope the new guy and I are going to get along. I'll tell you all about him in my next letter.

Love,
Johnny

P.S. Don't let them get you down. If Rob is really important to you, hold on to him.

October 14

Dear Sis,

My new roommate is named Howard Smith, and he's simply one of the greatest guys I've ever met. We've hit if off beautifully. We agree about everything. And he's a hard worker too. There won't be any goofing off this year in room 4–C. Howard's already so popular that the dorm's elected him representative to the school council.

87

He's from Alabama and his parents are poor. He's had a rough time, and if he hadn't won a scholarship he couldn't have made it to college. But he's plenty smart. And I can see that he really wants to make his family proud of him. He wants to go back home after he graduates and set up his own law practice. He thinks too many people are treated unjustly and he wants to devote his life to defending them.

I wonder what Howard would say if I told him what Dad wrote in his last letter to me. Dad was hopping mad because some of the black workers in his factory organized a union of their own. "Nothing satisfies them any more," he said. That's just the kind of thinking Howard feels he and his people are up against. Oh, I guess I forgot to tell you that Howard is black too.

But I suppose there's no changing Mom and Dad. I'll never understand why they can't just accept people as they are.

Anyway, I'm looking forward to being at home with you during Christmas vacation.

See you soon,
Love,
Johnny

October 30

Dear Sis,

It must have been awful for you. I can just imagine what Dad said and how he said it. "You know, Rob, personally we think you're pretty nice, and we really have nothing against our daughter's going out with you. But we must think of her position in this town. Many people are very narrow-minded here. And a lot of them feel that Jews are—well, how can I put it?"

And now Rob's really stopped seeing you? How depressed you must feel, Sis. I really sympathize. It's just not fair to you. But Mom and Dad don't care about being fair. They only care about what the neighbors think. How I wish I could do something for you and Rob. But you know as well as I that nothing *can* be done.

If it's any consolation, Howard, too, appreciates how bad you must feel. I hope you and Howard can meet some day. I'm sure you'll like each other. But I'm also sure there'll be trouble when Dad finds out I have a black roommate.

Well, it's bedtime. Howard's yelling for me to turn off the lights. We both have early classes tomorrow.

Write as soon as you can,
Johnny

November 12

Dear Sis,

I got a letter from Dad. He told me about his "saving you from the mistake of your life" by forcing you to give up Rob. He also said he's worried about the number of "foreigners and undesirables" moving into our neighborhood. And then he told me the "good news"—that he and Mom are driving up here for a visit in a couple of weeks. Now what do I do? Should I write them about Howard or just let them find out for themselves? Something tells me I'd better not surprise them. O.K., my mind's made up. Be ready for anything. I'm going to tell them!

Love,
Johnny

December 1

Dear Sis,

I just can't believe it's happening. You probably know Dad wrote me to say he's "shocked" about Howard. And he's ordered me to go to the Dean and ask him to change my roommate. He also said that if I don't go right away, I might as well forget about his paying my college expenses.

Sis, he means it! He's even threatened to write to the Dean himself. I'm so ashamed. What will the Dean think? What will all the guys in this dorm think of me? It isn't right of Dad to ask me to do this. Howard's a great roommate and the best guy there is. I'm sick and tired of Dad's hang-ups, and I really don't think I should give in to him.

But Sis, if he stops paying my tuition, I might have to drop out of college . . .

Well, I've got to decide right away.

Johnny

———————————

December 7

Dear Sis,

I . . .

OUT TO WIN

"And tomorrow," the coach's voice boomed, "I expect you to treat the members of the Frederick team with the same respect you would give any other team."

"Heck," Stewart said to himself, "just because there's a free Saturday on the schedule, does the coach have to invite *them* to Rexford?"

Stewart could well imagine what his father would say when he found out: "Is that why I spend $3,000 a year to send you to the best prep school in the East?"

And his mother would probably say, "I suppose those people will soon be expecting to *attend* Rexford—for free!"

"Any objections?" the coach demanded finally.

"Heck, yes!" Stewart whispered to himself. But he wouldn't dare say it out loud even though he knew he wasn't the only one there who felt that way.

He looked over at Roger. Their eyes met. Each knew the other was thinking the same thoughts. "That's O.K. Let 'em come. We'll show those black boys and Puerto Ricans who we are. We'll slaughter 'em."

The next day, there wasn't a cloud in the sky. It would be a perfect autumn afternoon—cold enough to show that winter was on the way but still warm enough for sitting comfortably in the stands.

Before Stewart had left for the game, his father had patted him on the back and said, "We know you'll win, Stewart. You're on the right side, the winning side." His mother didn't say anything. She only kissed him lightly on the cheek. But her look seemed to say, "I know you'll do us proud, Son." They were both out there now waiting for the game to begin.

Stewart knew that the key player on Frederick's team was its quarterback—"Ace," they called him. On defense, both Stewart and Roger knew that they had to get to this "Ace," even if it meant . . .

To Stewart's surprise, both sides seemed to have an equal number of rooters. The members of the Frederick team got as much of a roar of welcome when they ran out on the field as the Rexford team had. "Just you wait," said Stewart to himself. "We'll soon give you something to yell about."

But it wasn't going to be as easy as he thought. At the end of the first quarter, the score was 7–7. That quarterback, Ace, had called some pretty good plays and he had been hard to get to. They had been able to dump him only once. The beginning of the second quarter was even tighter.

Then Rexford's chance came. There was a mix-up in a call. Ace was left unprotected. Stewart and Roger got to him first. Roger hit him high and tried to get him down with an arm hold around his neck. Stewart collided head on with Ace and sent a sharp knee into his groin. In a flash, Rexford's whole defense piled on and Ace was buried.

When the whistle blew, the pack got up slowly. But one person was still left on the ground—Ace! And he wasn't moving at all.

Again the whistle blew, this time to stop the game. Stewart saw Frederick's coach and a doctor run out onto the field. After a while, a stretcher was brought out. Ace was very carefully lifted onto it and carried off the field. But Stewart hadn't been able to tell whether or not Ace had moved.

The game continued. Frederick put in a new quarterback. But he wasn't nearly clever enough. The plays he called just didn't click.

And something else was wrong with the Frederick team. It seemed to have lost its drive. It didn't

even seem to want to play. Stewart began to wonder if the team already knew something about Ace's condition.

One minute left to play. Stewart couldn't keep his thoughts from Ace. How serious *was* it? He hadn't really meant to hurt him badly—just enough to keep him out of the game for a while.

The final whistle blew. Rexford had won, 21–14. Back in the locker room, the Rexford team celebrated. Everyone joined in the back-slapping and laughter—everyone except Stewart.

"Hey, Stew," Roger yelled, "where're you hiding?" Stewart had gone out into the hall as soon as he had gotten out of his uniform. "Hey, Stew! The guys are looking for you. Come on back."

He found Stewart leaning against the wall, staring at the floor. "Wow," he said, "you really took care of that Ace guy. From what I hear, he won't be around to bother us for a long time."

Stewart looked up. "Do they know anything yet, Roger?"

"You know what they say. The only good one's a dead one . . ."

"What?"

" . . . And I hear he's half-dead already. Forget about him. Come on and celebrate."

Forget about him! Stewart wished he could. He hadn't meant to really hurt him, but he had gone too far.

Stewart had to get away. He needed time to think.

Outside, he followed his feet where they took him. He walked on and on, not knowing where, why, or for how long. Then he heard an ambulance siren. Only then did he realize that he had walked all the way to Rexford County Hospital.

In spite of himself he walked into the lobby. "Can I help you?" asked a voice behind the information window.

At first she couldn't understand what Stewart was saying. "Who?" she asked. "Speak up!"

"Ace—I mean Charles—Thompson's room, please," he finally managed to say clearly.

"Room 618—the elevator to your left."

Almost in a daze, Stewart found himself outside of Ace's hospital room. What was he doing there? What was he going to say. Then, he made his mind up and . . .

MY SISTER, THE $3.00 BILL

I guess a brother ought to stick up for his sister, even if she is a phony like my sister Peggy. Well, maybe "phony" is a little strong, but Peggy sure can act like a $3.00 bill at times. I should know. I'm Arnie, her brother.

She started in our very first day as transfer students at Franklin High. It could only have been Peggy those girls in the lunchroom were imitating. According to them, this is the way it went:

"Present, Mrs. Oates," she had answered when the teacher had called out her name. And the *way* she said it. You would have thought she was acting on a stage. Every eye was on her. I could just picture her sitting as stiff as she could at her desk, her eyes straight ahead, as if she were too grand to look at anyone.

And the way she was dressed that day—the way she always *tries* to dress—like a fashion model! Most of the students wore sweatshirts and sandals. No wonder she made everyone so uncomfortable.

Then on the third or fourth day of school I overheard her talking to a couple of girls. "Well, it was a last-minute decision. Mother and Father didn't really want to move away, but Father knows how important he is to the company, so he agreed to come to Lewisville to help out . . ."

Darn right, Mother and Father didn't want to come to Lewisville. Dad had a nice job back in Bakersfield. But his company had already laid off a lot of people, and Dad had to go where they sent him or get laid off like the rest.

That was only the beginning. Peggy really laid it on those girls.

"Our new terrace is not nearly large enough," she said. *Terrace!* Why we hardly have a front porch. And then she told them we never ate dinner before *eight*. Heck, we always eat at six, like everyone else, unless Mom forgets to unfreeze the chops, which happens once in a while. But nothing can be ordinary for Peggy. Why, she'll never call anything by its regular name if she can use a French word instead. Where does she get her ideas?

We've got pretty nice parents—plain, but solid. It was sure tough on them to leave Bakersfield after living there for 30 years. But I must admit, Peggy didn't make it any easier on them. How she complained. "I can't leave all my friends behind." Who was she kidding? Peggy couldn't really call a single person in Bakersfield her friend.

And did she give my folks fits when they were

looking for a new place here in town! My parents have never really had much money. Anyway, they would never think of spending more money than they should just to impress people. Naturally, Peggy pestered them to get one of those huge apartments in the new high rise on Denton Place. You can imagine how much a three-bedroom apartment costs in that building!

She finally had to settle for the house we found on Market Street. It's a nice little place. And I don't mind if I have to sleep on a sofa bed in the living room. Did Peggy make a fuss about that, though: "Mother, you can't be serious about taking this place. If Arnie sleeps in the living room, where will I entertain my friends?" Her *friends!*

But things have a way of catching up with people. And Peggy eventually got herself into a bind. It happened when she finally met a boy she thought was good enough for her. His name is Tom, and he is new in town too. I was sitting close enough to hear bits and pieces of what she was telling him one day outside on the school lawn. Boy, how I wish I had had a tape recorder with me!

"Father's country club friends . . ."

"The garden party . . ."

"The society page . . ."

"French Provincial furniture . . ."

She went on and on like that. I wouldn't have believed it if I hadn't heard it myself. But the best part came when Tom asked her for a date.

"I'll come over to your house tonight and pick you up. How about eight o'clock? And by the way, what's your address?" he asked.

"Oh, no, Tom. I'm not going straight home this evening. Why don't I just meet you in front of the movie?" You should have seen Peggy's face!

You think that's the end of the story? Not on your life! About 7:15 that evening I was on my street corner talking to one of my friends. And who do I see walking towards me? That's right—Tom.

"Hi, Arnie. I'm supposed to meet Peggy in front of the movie at eight, but I was running early so I thought I'd just take a chance and drop by. Is she at home?"

I tried to keep a straight face. "Oh, she's home all right."

"Which house is it?"

I almost choked with laughter as I pointed it out. I watched him go up to the door. Then he hesitated and looked back at me as if he thought I might have been pulling his leg. Finally, he rang the doorbell. As I walked toward the house, Peggy opened the door. I heard her say . . .

A WORLD OF HER OWN

May's life had always been full and exciting. She had wonderful friends and they all went to fabulous places together. At least, that's what May told everyone. The trouble was, none of it was true. And long ago, everyone had stopped believing her.

Then one day May really tripped herself up. It all began in the school cafeteria when she was telling some of her friends: "And after dinner, we're all going out to that new play and then to Don's party—and you know Don's parties . . ."

But before she could finish, Beth had interrupted her. "Oh, are you going to that play too? Now I'll get to meet some of those marvelous friends of yours."

Oh well, May was sure she could find some way to cover up her lie when the time came. Still, the way Beth had said *friends* had sent a chill through her. Were the girls on to her, May wondered.

Deep down, she knew they were. People just never asked her out any more. Now May was a very lonely girl.

And she would have given anything to be in Beth's place, or anybody else's. She was tired of pretending and imagining, tired of building one lie upon another, tired of spending Saturday nights alone in her room. Sometimes she dreamed of running away. She wouldn't miss anyone, and no one would miss her. Her foster parents certainly wouldn't care if she left. She would start a new life somewhere—a *real* life. But May knew she'd never have the courage to do it.

That night, May felt more unhappy than ever. For a while she watched television, but all the programs seemed boring. So she turned off the set and picked up her latest copy of *The Now Girl*. It was her favorite magazine, and also the place where she got many ideas for her make-believe life.

An ad she had never paid much attention to before caught her eye. Now it seemed to be speaking just to her.

ARE YOU TIRED OF SPENDING EVERY SATURDAY NIGHT ALONE? Longing to find the just-right date or mate? Let our computer do the finding. It's scientific and it's sound. Our computer's a real Cupid. So just fill out the blank below and send it to us along with five dollars. We promise that very soon you'll find that Saturday night's the *liveliest* night of the week!

May hesitated for an instant, then she thought, "Why not! What do I have to lose!"

She hurried to her desk and began to fill out the blank. Name . . . Address . . . Color of hair . . . Color of eyes . . .

AGE: "Maybe . . . a couple of extra years. Everyone thinks I run around with an older crowd." She wrote *19* in the space.

HEIGHT: "Five feet eight . . . No!" She quickly crossed it out. "Who wants to go out with a giraffe? If I slouch a little I could pass for . . ." She put down *5'5"*.

WEIGHT: "I'll just have to stop eating all those sweets. If I stick to a diet for the next three weeks . . ." *125 pounds,* she wrote.

INTERESTS: Right away she wrote in *books and good music*. "After all," she thought, "I do want to meet a *refined* boy." But then she thought she ought to try to appeal to the outdoors type as well. So she added *swimming* and *tennis*.

May reread all that she had written. She was pleased with her description of herself. Then she decided to send along a photo. She found a print of the picture taken for her yearbook. She knew it was quite flattering. Then she put everything into an envelope, addressed it and added a stamp.

For the first time in many days she felt good. Now she was sure her life was going to be different. Already her mind was full of thoughts about what she was going to tell Beth and the other girls. "Well, it happened so suddenly. He's a friend of Dick's from New York City, and he's so *cultured* and such a *gentleman*. You can't imagine all the things he tells me about. I think he's in love with me . . ."

May felt light on her feet as she went out to mail the letter. She kept picturing the sort of boys who were going to answer. "Six feet tall—champion swimmer—likes to camp out." Well, maybe camping wasn't for her, but she could get used to it if she had to . . .

Or maybe there would be even better responses. "Blond, blue eyes—likes classical and semi-classical music—reads a lot . . ." That was the kind of boy she really would like to meet.

It was beginning to get dark when she set out to mail her letter. As she walked along, she saw a familiar figure at the other end of the block. Beth! And who was the other person? Her date. They must be on the way to the play. And now they were only half-a-block away! There was no time to lose. What was she to do?

New lies began to spring into her mind. "Should I say my date got sick? That my foster-mother made

me stay home?" All of a sudden, May felt she just couldn't tell any more lies. "No, it won't work."

She began to panic. "Away! I must get away! That doorway . . ." May pressed herself into it as tightly as she could. The darkness would hide her, she hoped.

Then, she heard what sounded like laughter. What was Beth laughing at? Had she seen her?

They were passing her now. May pressed ever more tightly into the shadows. "Thank goodness!" She sighed with relief. "They didn't see . . ."

"Hi, May. You'll have a hard time seeing the play from that doorway!" Beth laughed and passed on with her date.

May stood there for a long while. Her eyes were filled with tears. Finally, she stirred. She saw that she had let the letter fall to the ground. She reached down and picked it up.

"Lies, lies, lies," she whispered to herself. "What good did they ever do me?" A look of disgust crossed her face. "I'm just going to tear this thing up . . ."

She hesitated a moment, looked at the letter again, and . . .

JUST LIKE YOUR SISTER

Audrey knew this would be the most important day of her life. But would it be the beginning of a new and better life, or . . . She didn't dare finish her thought.

The face of the kitchen clock was so stained from the leaks in the ceiling that Audrey could hardly make out the time. Six o'clock—still an hour and a half before she would be able to make her phone call. For the hundredth time that day, she searched her sweater pocket for the piece of paper with the number. It was still there.

Audrey's mother was at the stove preparing supper. Suddenly, she turned around and said sharply, "Audrey, don't just sit there doing nothing! The devil finds work for idle hands. Have you finished your homework?"

Audrey was shaken out of her thoughts. "Yes, ma'am," she dragged out the words. She didn't like lying to her mother. "But what was the point of studying?" she thought. By this time tomorrow evening, she would probably be miles and miles away from this house and everything she hated about it.

Once again, she reached into her pocket. Then she stood up nervously and walked into the next room. Maybe Baby was awake. How nice it would be to play with her one more time. But no, Baby was sound asleep.

Back in the kitchen, she checked the clock again. Only 6:10. How slowly time was moving. Her mother was still busy at the stove. Soon the usual supper of cabbage and turnip greens with pork fat would be steaming on the table. "How did that woman always have so much energy after a long day's work," Audrey wondered.

"The good Lord meant that we should have one big meal a day," her mother often said. And somehow, "the Lord" always provided it, whether money was scarce or not.

"Well," her mother said as she turned to her, "how about setting the table."

Audrey obeyed silently. Out came the cracked, chipped dishes from the cupboard, the patched, worn tablecloth from the drawer. How depressing they were. How depressing it was to be so poor.

Suddenly, Audrey noticed an unopened letter on the cupboard shelf. It was addressed to her mother. By looking at the handwriting, she knew it was from Bernadine. Across the front of the envelope her mother had written "Return to sender."

Audrey finished setting the table and sat down,

but her heart was beating quickly. She wanted so much to say something about the letter, but she didn't dare. Her mother would only say, "The Lord never meant that girl to be my daughter!" She'd be angry at Audrey for bringing the subject up.

It had been nearly three years since she'd last seen her sister. How she missed her, and how much she needed her at times.

"You'd better feed Baby now." Her mother handed her a bowl of hot cereal. "I'm running late, and I want to be on time for prayer meeting."

Audrey felt like yelling at the top of her voice: "Stop calling her Baby. Give her a name. She's Bernardine's baby and she's almost three years old."

Audrey entered the tiny room with the cereal in her hand. She looked around. How happy she was going to be to get out of this place. Those few broken sticks of furniture. That narrow bed she used to share with her mother *and* Bernardine. She'd never live crowded like this again, she vowed to herself.

Baby awoke and started laughing. She was always glad to see Audrey. She was such a strange child. She never cried. Audrey bent over her and hugged her tenderly.

"Baby's the wage of sin," Audrey's mother often said, "or else she would've talked by now. The Lord knows what He's doing when He gives us our cross to bear."

It was true that Baby couldn't talk. And she hadn't yet learned to walk, either. But Baby was good, and she was so lovable . . . Tears came to Audrey's eyes as she lifted a spoonful of cereal to Baby's mouth. She would miss her terribly when she left. Who would care for her and love her the way she did?

Poor Baby hadn't had a very good start. Audrey began thinking about Baby and Bernardine. Four years earlier Bernardine had run away from home with a man she hardly knew. A year later she came back looking thin, tired, and kind of old. The man had wandered off and left her with a tiny baby.

But Bernardine didn't stay at home very long. One day she just disappeared again. No one knew where she had gone. A neighbor said that Bernardine had run off with another man and was living in a nearby town. Another said that he had seen her in a nightclub with some pretty fast company. And there were other stories . . .

"If Bernardine has sent a letter, she must be in real trouble," Audrey thought to herself. "Maybe I ought to open it myself and . . ." She heard the oven door slam. Supper was ready. Audrey gave Baby her last spoonful and hurried into the kitchen. Six thirty-five, the clock showed. Another 55 minutes.

Audrey's mother was already sitting at the table. Her head was bowed. She was ready to say the blessing. Audrey dropped down into her chair and lowered her eyes. Her mother was "running late" but she had to give a full five minutes to the Lord. When Audrey finally heard, "Thank You Lord for all You have given us," she sighed with relief. She would have liked to have said, "That's a laugh!"

They ate in silence. When they were finished, Audrey's mother said another blessing. She always said one before and after every meal. "Thanks before and thanks after!" Audrey sneered to herself. "And thanks for what? For misery and silence?"

Audrey cleared the table and began to wash the dishes in the cracked sink. A roach ran across the wall in front of her. No matter how clean her mother kept the place, there were always roaches. "Only another 25 minutes," she whispered to herself as she glanced at the clock.

Her mother came back into the room in her only good dress. "Tonight I'll be coming home later than usual," she said. "I promised Sister Mary I'd give her a hand with some things." She left without another word.

"Good!" thought Audrey, "that will give me enough time . . ." She went over the whole thing in her mind. At seven-thirty, she was to call Martin at his hotel. He'd tell her where to meet him, and they'd decide where to go from there.

"Don't bring anything with you, Babe. I'll get you anything you need," Martin had said. "Thank goodness he'd said that," thought Audrey. She had nothing to bring.

Audrey had to keep telling herself she was doing the right thing. Martin had been very kind to her, and he made her feel important. He treated her like a full-grown woman. But she really hadn't known him very long. Was she going to make the same mistake Bernardine had made?

"No," she said to herself. "It isn't the same thing at all. I can take care of myself." Deep down, Audrey felt that any kind of life would be better than the one she had.

It was now twenty minutes past seven. Still ten minutes to go. She'd walk down to the hall phone now. She wanted to make sure no one would be using it.

But just as she was about to step out into the hall, she heard an unfamiliar noise coming from the apartment. It was Baby. And she was crying—crying for the first time! Audrey ran back into Baby's room and took the child in her arms. "Why is she crying? Does she understand that I'm leaving?" Audrey asked herself.

"Don't worry, honey," she began to soothe Baby. "I'll be back for you, I promise. I won't let you stay here. I'll get some money and take you to the best doctor in . . ." Baby stopped crying. Audrey put her back into her crib. Audrey realized with a start that it must be seven-thirty.

She rushed out the door and down the three flights of stairs to the telephone.

No one was there. She put her dime in the slot, took the paper out of her pocket, and dialed the number carefully. The moment had come!

Her hand was shaking. Six, seven, eight rings. Finally, she heard a voice. "Hotel Albin."

Still out of breath, Audrey could hardly get out the words: "Could I . . . speak to Mr. . . . Martin Johnson, please?" Her throat felt dry and tight.

She waited. Her heart was pounding. Then she heard the voice say, "I'm sorry. Mr. Johnson checked out of the hotel about noon today."

"He . . . what?" Audrey cried out in disbelief. But the only reply she heard was a click as the phone was hung up on the other end.

For a while she stood there, too shaken to move. Tears streamed down her face. Finally she started up the rickety old staircase. Each step was torture. Would she never, never get away from these smelly hallways?

At the top of the stairs, she realized that Baby was crying again. Audrey ran in and took her up in her arms. "Don't cry . . . I won't be leaving after all," she sobbed. And she pressed her cheek against the child's until their tears mingled.

After a while, Baby quieted down. She seemed to be smiling. "I'll always be with you," Audrey whispered. Then she tucked Baby into her crib and walked quietly out of the room.

In the kitchen she broke down completely. Never had she felt so desperate before. For a moment she thought of running down the stairs into the streets—running and running until . . . But where would she run to? Martin had been her only hope. Now he'd let her down. He was no better than the man who had ruined her sister! Maybe her mother was right. Maybe all men are rotten. It was a good thing she had found out now . . . But Martin . . . He had seemed so different . . .

Suddenly, Audrey realized that there were foot-steps on the stairs. Slow footsteps. She held her breath. The sound stopped just outside her door.

Was her mother back from prayer meeting so soon? Was a neighbor coming to pay a call?

There was a light knock at the door. Then, two ideas flashed across Audrey's mind, one after the other: It might be . . . Martin. Or it might even be . . . Bernardine!

A second knock. Louder this time. Baby started to cry again. Audrey hurried over to the door and opened it. She let out a startled cry as her heart skipped a beat. There standing before her was . . .

MY SON, THE DOCTOR

That morning, Luis had been graduated from college. When he got home he saw that the living-room furniture had already been cleared for the family celebration.

"My son, the doctor!" cried his mother as he walked in. She almost threw him off balance as she kissed him happily. Aunt Rosa looked up from her vacuuming and smiled approvingly. Neither of them seemed to notice how serious he looked.

"Not a doctor yet," he said, his eyes lowered. "Medical school takes at least four more years and . . ." He interrupted himself suddenly. "Momma, please sit down. I have something important to tell you . . ."

"Who has time to talk now?" She took up her broom again. "And Aunt Rosa and I still have cooking to do."

"At least let me help you finish," he offered, graver than ever.

"Does a doctor sweep floors?" said Aunt Rosa. And both she and his mother burst out laughing.

"Go to your room and keep your nose in your books till everyone arrives," said Momma.

In his room, sitting on the edge of his bed, Luis felt confused and scared. The Peace Corps application was lying on his desk, filled out and ready to be mailed. It would *never* make any sense to his mother, he was sure.

"What was he doing with his life anyway?" he wondered for the hundredth time. Most of it had already been spent in school. Now he had to spend another eight years of it studying medicine. And his family would keep on sacrificing for him until he was through.

He needed time to think—about his future role in society, about the profession to which they all wanted him to devote his life, about certain hopes and dreams apart from his family, his neighborhood and his friends. "After two years," he kept repeating to himself, "I can always come back and finish school."

And in the Peace Corps, he thought, there is a chance for me to do something *now* for needy people. The world is so full of problems. And there are so many places, even in this "Land of Opportunity," where people are desperate for help. But could Momma ever accept the idea that there are more important things to do than go to school?

Luis began pacing the floor again, as he had been pacing for the past two weeks. Worst of all, he could not put thoughts of his dead father from his mind.

How hard it had been for the whole family before they had left the Island. But had it been much easier for them since? When they arrived on the mainland, none of them could speak English. Luis's father soon learned that there were few good jobs to be had, especially by Puerto Ricans who speak little English. Even dishwasher and counterman jobs were hard to find. The poor man had finally worked himself to death trying to hold down three different jobs to make ends meet.

In spite of such hardship, Luis's mother had scrimped and saved enough so that he could finish high school and go on to college. With a large family and a house to look after, she had sweated nights over other people's laundry. In all those years he could remember her getting only one new dress. That one she got for his cousin's wedding. And she wouldn't waste a penny on her own medical care if she could manage with aspirin. "Don't worry about me," she would say to him. "I'll have plenty of time to rest later. You'll be my doctor then, Luis."

Aunt Rosa, too, had given something out of her weekly paychecks towards his education. In fact, every member of the family had helped in his or her own way, though there was never very much to give. A Puerto Rican family works together. And now Luis could hear them arriving downstairs—Uncle Tony, Aunt Maria, Uncle Juan, Cousin Dolores—each of them sharing in his mother's pleasure and rejoicing in his future success. How could he disappoint them now?

"Luis, the family . . . come . . ." He heard his mother's voice as if from another world.

He delayed as long as he could. "She *has* to understand," he said once again to himself. "She *has* to accept my decision. I must live my own life, make my own choices. But I would do anything not to hurt her, not to hurt any of them . . ."

He entered the living room to the applause of all his relatives. His mother came forward and took him by the arm. Tears filled her eyes. "I present to you my son . . . the future Doctor Luis Rodriguez."

"Speech, speech!" cried Uncle Tony. "Let the great man speak for himself." The room went still with anticipation. All eyes were upon him. Luis let go of his mother's arm, then he slowly looked from one eager face to another.

"Dear family . . ." For an instant, his voice failed him. "Dear family, I want you to know how much I love Momma . . . Aunt Rosa . . . each of you . . . I would never do anything that would make you unhappy . . ."

"A little louder, Luis," called old Aunt Maria. "You're almost whispering."

Luis cleared his throat and . . .

HONOR THY FATHER AND THY MOTHER

"No. Sorry. I can't leave now. Who knows what they'll be like when they get back here."

"But Tony," insisted the voice on the other end of the phone, "These people from State College are announcing their decision this afternoon. They'll probably want to talk to you. They'll probably want to see you act again. This might be your only chance for . . ."

"I know all that, Ross. And I appreciate your calling . . ." Tony's voice could not hide the bitterness he felt. That drama scholarship meant the world to him. Of course, his parents hadn't saved any money to send him to college, and he probably wouldn't be able to go without a scholarship. "There'll be other years, Ross. I'll just have to wait a while, that's all."

"Oh, don't give me that, Tony. Who do you think you're kidding? If I had to put up with a father and mother like yours . . . It isn't fair to you!"

"That's enough, Ross! My parents are having a rough time. They do the best they can. Anyway, I won't have you talking about them that way."

"O.K., fella, it's your problem—but I hate to see your future going down the drain because . . ."

"That's not your affair, Ross. I'll be seeing you." Tony quickly hung up the receiver. He felt he had to do something—throw the telephone across the room, yell, slam a door, anything. Why couldn't anyone understand?

Sure his parents were hard to take. But they *were* his parents, and he *did* care about them. There had been times when he could talk to them. But now they were . . .

But he didn't want to say it, not even to himself. Anyway, there were the kids to think of. He had to stop all this feeling sorry for himself. Lynn and Willie would be marching in soon, hungry as ever. They'd be expecting their dinner on the table whether Mother was back or not.

Just then, the front door flew open and Lynn burst in, shouting, "We're starving." She walked into the kitchen, followed by Willie. Tony knew what she'd say next.

"That lunch you made us was for the birds. We're getting awfully tired of jelly sandwiches. That was the third time this week . . ."

Tony tried to look cheerful. "Yeah, but I gave you two different kinds of jelly. Don't say that isn't something different."

"Oh, some joke. Why don't you go on TV?"

"Sure," Willie added, "and then we'll have enough money for *three* kinds of jelly."

It wasn't really funny, but they laughed anyway. They enjoyed being silly together, though their jokes wouldn't make sense to anyone else.

Tony, Lynn, and Willie had shared many moments like these, especially in the last year. They didn't have much else in their lives.

Tony felt more like a parent than a big brother. He did the best he could to keep them happy. But sometimes it wasn't easy. Whenever he'd arrange for them to do something special, one of the kids would always ask, "Can we all do it together?"

"Uh, uh," Tony would say, "Dad's got to work late," or "Mom's got some extra shopping to do . . ."

The children weren't fooled. Sometimes they got mad and sometimes they were hurt, but on the whole, they accepted things. And they trusted Tony to keep things going.

Tony looked up at the kitchen clock. Five-thirty. Mom and Dad should be home any minute now. But what if it was going to be one of those nights they didn't come home at all?

"Let's give them another 15 minutes," he said to the kids, who were already seated at the table. "Come on—get rid of those long faces. You won't starve to death in 15 minutes."

Tony hurried to the stove. He couldn't let the soup boil over this time. To keep busy, he stirred the spaghetti sauce once again. His hands were tense. "What's it going to be like tonight?" he kept asking himself. "Oh, please God, let everything be all right tonight."

"Five forty-five. No use," he thought out loud. "O.K., kids, let's eat," he called to them. "Hey, Willie, wash up! You know better than that."

The soup tasted pretty good, even if he did say so himself. But Tony had had lots of cooking practice. Willie was soon reaching for a second bowlful. Then they heard the sound of loud, angry voices coming from the hallway. The three dropped their spoons and looked at one another. They knew now what kind of evening it would turn out to be.

"Go on. It was your fault. I didn't break the stuff," their mother was now shouting across the living room. "If you wouldn't have opened your mouth to him, he wouldn't have thrown us out . . ."

"He had no right . . . I was gonna pay for the mess," their father yelled back at her.

The noise of their argument continued for a few moments, then stopped suddenly.

"Oh, hello, sweeties!" Tony's mother now stood smiling at the kitchen door. Her hair and clothes were messy looking, her makeup was all smeared. "How are my babies?" She leaned over Willie first and planted a wet kiss on his cheek. Then she stumbled over to Lynn and kissed her too. Lynn had wanted to turn her face away. The smell of whiskey made her sick. But she couldn't hurt her mother's feelings.

"And how's our Tony tonight?" their Dad asked in a big, cheery voice.

"Our Tony! Was that supposed to make up for their being late? For their acting this way?" Tony asked himself bitterly.

"Oh, it's dinner time already," said Mom.

"Goodness, how I lose track of time . . . Thanks for getting things started, Tony. I'll go get the . . ."

"No, Mother, you don't need to . . ." Tony said. But she was already rattling among the things on the kitchen counter. In a minute, she returned, empty-handed. "I'm so sorry. I can't seem to find the . . ." Suddenly, she had to catch hold of the table to support herself. "I'm a little dizzy," she said with a weak laugh.

"It's O.K., Mother, I'll manage . . ." But no. She was back at the stove. For a moment, Tony turned around to see what had happened to his father. There he was, already sprawled on the living room sofa. He'd probably sleep it off there till morning.

Crash! All three jumped up from their chairs. The spaghetti lay in messy globs all over the kitchen floor! "Oh dear," their mother began to wail, "I can't do anything any more."

Tony quickly found the mop and began to clean up the mess. The children just stood in the middle of the floor, too shaken to move. All they could do was stare at their mother. She was stomping around in the gooey mess, crying louder and louder, the way alcohol always made her cry.

Finally she said, "I'm just no good tonight. I'm going to bed. I'll get out of your way. I'll be all right later. I'm so sorry, children . . ." Somehow, she managed to make her way up the stairs.

Willie looked at Tony. Then he ran out of the house. Lynn put her head down on the table and began crying. Tony looked around him at the mess in the kitchen and began to feel more and more hopeless. The poor kids—to have to see this, night after night. Would it never change? No, it was only going to get worse.

"Hey fella!" Tony looked up. It was Ross, standing in the kitchen doorway. "You did it! You got the scholarship!"

For a moment, he couldn't believe his ears. "You gotta be kidding."

"Kidding! They were so impressed that they awarded you a scholarship without a second audition."

Tony let go. "Wowee!"

"They even arranged for your train fare. The new term starts early at State, and you've got to be there by the end of the month. Mr. Jones, the college representative, will be here soon with all the forms for you to sign. Isn't that the greatest thing . . ."

Another crash—this time from upstairs—followed by a loud curse. Ross knew it could only be Tony's mother.

Ross began looking all about him. Sticky spaghetti was spilled all over the floor. Lynn, her head on the table, was crying her eyes out. And in the living room, Tony's father, snoring and gurgling, had slipped half-way off the sofa onto the floor. "Oh, no!" Ross gasped.

"There! Now you see for yourself why I can't go."

"Can't go? Are you crazy? Tony, what are you doing to yourself?" Ross began to plead. "Are you going to spend the rest of your days baby-sitting for your brother and sister and playing nursemaid to two drunken parents? You've got your own life to live. You've just got to get away from here. State's giving you the chance. Please, Tony, tell Mr. Jones 'yes' when he comes."

Tony didn't answer. The room was very quiet, except for his mother's grumbling upstairs. Tony looked at his father—then at Lynn.

Just then, the doorbell rang. They knew who it must be, but no one made a move to answer the door. The bell rang again. Ross walked to the door and opened it. There stood Mr. Jones. He slowly took in the scene around him.

Tony looked up and said, ". . .

CLOSING UP THE OPEN-ENDS

MIND YOUR OWN BUSINESS

THINKING ABOUT THE STORY

1. Would you describe Stan as a "dope addict"? Give your reasons.
2. What clues show that Stan was on drugs?
3. At what point in the story is Bill sure of Stan's problem? When were you sure of his problem?
4. What kind of home life do you think Stan has? Do you think Bill's home life is the same? Find any sentences in the story that might support your answers.
5. Where might Stan go for help with his drug problem? What kinds of jobs are available in the areas of drug control and rehabilitation?

THINKING ABOUT THE ENDING

1. Below are some endings for this story. Which endings seem more possible than the

rest? Be able to give reasons for your
choices.
  (a) Bill calls Stan's mother to tell about
      her son's problem.
  (b) Bill decides to wait and do nothing.
  (c) Bill is angry with Stan for hitting him.
      He decides to drop him as a friend.
  (d) Bill calls the coach. Together, they
      work out a plan.
  (e) Bill calls the police.
2. What other endings are possible?

RUN, BABY, RUN

THINKING ABOUT THE STORY

1. What do we know of Harris' early life?
2. Why is Jim an important person to Harris?
3. Why did Jim tell Harris, "Think as much of
   yourself as you want others to think of you."?
   What are some other sayings similar to this
   one?
4. What is meant by "Working Main Street?"
5. How is the word **ghetto** used in this story?
   What are some other kinds of ghettos?
6. Besides law enforcement, what other jobs
   might appeal to a person interested in serving
   his community? Would you be interested in
   any of these careers? Why?

THINKING ABOUT THE ENDING

1. What important decision must Harris make?
2. Why does he hesitate to make this decision?
3. What do you think he finally decides to do?
4. Is this decision in character with the kind of
   person Harris is? Why or why not?

BUT I DIDN'T KNOW

THINKING ABOUT THE STORY

1. Why does Marge like going to Hillside Park?
2. Why do you think Pete goes there?
3. Why do Pete and Marge become friends so quickly?
4. Some of the following statements are made by Marge and some by Pete. Try to identify the speaker of each statement.

   "I'm bored! I'm bored."

   "I'd be no fun at a dance."

   "Nothing to do . . . same old stuff."

   "It's horrible to be lame."

   "Sometimes you have to get interested in things."

   What do these statements tell us about the two people?
5. When did you guess that Pete is lame?
6. What clues are given in the story to help you discover that Pete is crippled?
7. Pete in this story and Tom in "Let George Do It" are both loners. In what ways are they alike? How are they different?
8. Think of someone you know who is physically handicapped. What job opportunities do you think are open to such a person?

THINKING ABOUT THE ENDING

1. Write one brief answer that Marge would give Pete in each of the following situations:
   (a) She agrees to go out with him
   (b) She decides not to go and makes up an excuse
   (c) She decides to be truthful with him and turns him down

2. Prepare an imaginary telephone conversation between Marge and Pete, using any of the situations described in question 1.

NOT LIKE JEFF

THINKING ABOUT THE STORY

1. From the following quotations, which boy is being described, Jeff or Stevie?
   (a) "Not even a B average."
   (b) ". . . he's pulling an A average . . ."
   (c) "A real movie star."
   (d) ". . . struggles along in school."
   (e) "Who knows what's bothering him this time!"
   (f) ". . . such a kind boy."
   (g) ". . . we ought to encourage him."
2. How do you think Jeff feels about his mother? How do you think Stevie feels about his mother? How do you think the two brothers feel about each other?
3. Is competition among brothers and sisters worthwhile? Why or why not?
4. How do parents affect the career choice of their children?

THINKING ABOUT THE ENDING

1. Imagine that Stevie has come down the steps in a very angry mood. Then, write the dialogue that might be spoken by Stevie and his mother.
2. Imagine that Jeff has overheard Stevie and mother. What would Jeff say to his mother? to Stevie?

WENDY

1. What words might Mr. Gilmore use to describe Wendy? to describe himself?
2. What words might Wendy use to describe herself? to describe her father?
3. Mr. Gilmore feels that school should teach "American history, science and math," and not encourage students to become involved in issues. Do you agree? Explain.
4. Mr. Gilmore says that teachers do not like Wendy's **attitude.** What do you think the teachers mean?
5. If you had your choice would you rather live in Stevie's home ("Not Like Jeff") or in Wendy's home? Why?

THINKING ABOUT THE ENDING

1. Have you decided who is right and who is wrong? Good! Now finish the letter to Mr. Gilmore. Bring it to class.

ONCE UPON A TIME

THINKING ABOUT THE STORY

1. Why is "Once Upon a Time" a good title for this story?
2. What other title could you give this story?
3. Do you think Mary's parents did an honest job in preparing her to face life? Explain your answer.

4. If you were Mary's parent, what would you have told her?
5. What kind of parents do you think the young man has?
6. How does Mary really feel about her parents?
7. What are some ways in which Mary, Jeff and Wendy are alike?

THINKING ABOUT THE ENDING

1. How do you think the story ends?
2. Imagine that you are Mary's mother or father. On a sheet of paper, write an ending the way they would write it.

LETTERS TO A SOLDIER

THINKING ABOUT THE STORY

1. Over what period of time does this story take place?
2. What changes take place in Gloria over that period of time?
3. Why does Gloria join the S.W.I.?
4. What changes take place in Bob over this period of time?
5. Who probably shows a greater change, Gloria or Bob? Why?
6. Why is Clara important to the story?
7. Gloria wrote the following things to Bob:
   (a) "Just a short while ago I thought all peaceniks were kooks."
   (b) "We can devote the future to helping other people."

(c) "That wonderful postman brought me another letter from you today."

(d) "Nobody here seems to notice that the world is falling apart."

Arrange these statements in their proper order to show how Gloria's ideas about life have changed.

THINKING ABOUT THE ENDING

1. Will Gloria agree to end her relationship with Bob? Be ready to explain your answer.
2. Briefly list two possible endings on a sheet of paper. Then, choose one of these endings and expand it into a letter answering Bob's letter.

HE IS NOT DEAD

THINKING ABOUT THE STORY

1. What are three things in the story that led you to suspect that Eric is part of the American Nazi Party?
2. Why does the girl continue to go out with Eric?
3. Is it likely that she can change Eric's beliefs? Explain your answer.
4. Is it possible that Eric could change her beliefs? Why or why not?
5. Who would buy these bumper stickers, Clara ("Letters to a Soldier") or Eric?
    (a) White Is Right
    (b) Make Love, Not War
    (c) America, Love It or Leave It
    (d) America, Change It or Get Out

1. Complete the entry for December 12 on a sheet of paper.

LET GEORGE DO IT

THINKING ABOUT THE STORY

1. Why is Tom happy to have George as a friend?
2. In what ways does Tom change because of this friendship?
3. Why did George choose Tom as a friend?
4. Why do you think George dropped his other friends?
5. Who has more to gain from this friendship, George or Tom? Why?
6. If you could choose only one friend, would you pick Tom or George? Why?
7. Decide which friendship might be more lasting:
   George and Tom
      or
   Stan and Bill ("Mind Your Own Business")

THINKING ABOUT THE ENDING

1. On a sheet of paper, write three possible endings for this story, starting in this way:
   (a) Tom . . .
   (b) George . . .
   (c) The principal . . .

WILLIE LAWSON FOR PRESIDENT

1. Why is it so important for Willie Lawson to be chosen President of the Student Council? Would the same reason apply today in your school? Why or why not?
2. We sometimes hear of people being "caught in the middle" of something. Willie found himself "caught in the middle." Explain why.
3. Judging from the headlines it ran after the school election, the local newspaper has what attitude towards Willie's victory?
4. If the newspaper had been neutral in its coverage of this event, what might the headlines have said?
5. In what ways could you compare Willie and Harris ("Run, Baby, Run")?
6. What jobs are available through politics or political appointment? What might be helpful to you in preparing for a career in politics?

THINKING ABOUT THE ENDING

1. Under what circumstances must Willie make his most important decision?
2. What are the possible choices he has?
3. Make a decision for Willie.
   - (a) How might Allan react to this decision?
   - (b) How might Tyrone react to this decision?
   - (c) How might the school principal react to this decision?

THE MAN WITH
THE CIGAR

THINKING ABOUT THE STORY

1. Why is it important for Paul's team to win this game?
2. What events in the story cause Paul to be upset?
3. Why do you think the man with the cigar is in the hospital waiting room?
4. Why are Chip and Matt important to the story?
5. How does responsibility play an important part in the stories "Run, Baby, Run", "Willie Lawson For President", and "The Man With The Cigar"?
6. Name some job opportunities that exist at a hospital. What qualities or special skills might be necessary for each of the following: laboratory technician; nurse; nurse's aid; dietician; druggist; x-ray technician; ambulance driver.

THINKING ABOUT THE ENDING

1. Decide whether these statements are true or false. Be prepared to defend your answers.
    (a) The man with the cigar causes Paul to lose the game.
    (b) Paul keeps the money to pay the hospital bills.
    (c) Paul keeps the money and later enters the university and agrees to meet the man again.
    (d) Paul grabs the man with the cigar and calls the police.

WALK PROUD, BE PROUD

THINKING ABOUT THE STORY

1. What does the title "Walk Proud, Be Proud" mean?
2. How does Pat feel about Linda?
3. If you were Pat, would you feel the same way? Why or why not?
4. Do you think that Linda really wants to be friends with Pat? Give reasons for your answer.
5. Pat's mother told her never to accept charity. Did the mother really believe what she told Pat? Support your answer.
6. Near the end of the story, Linda's mother says, "I guess I handled that very badly." What else could Linda's mother have done?
7. Pat wants to be a ballet performer. Would you be interested in a career in music, art, dance or the theatre? Why?

THINKING ABOUT THE ENDING

1. Finish the story. Keep in mind the way Pat was brought up and the way Pat feels at the very end of the story.

PLAY THE GAME

THINKING ABOUT THE STORY

1. Why is Aunt Alma dissatisfied with Bruce? List the things she doesn't like.

2. Words like **family, Mayflower,** and **cultural enrichment** are very important to Aunt Alma. What do they tell us about her?
3. Is Bruce right in describing her as a snob? Why or why not?
4. Another word that might describe Aunt Alma is **bigot.** Why?
5. Why does the family want to please Aunt Alma?
6. What does the term "playing the game" mean?
7. Could the term "playing the game" be applied to anyone in Pat's story ("Walk Proud, Be Proud")? Explain.

THINKING ABOUT THE ENDING

1. Is Bruce willing to "play the game"? Why or why not?
2. Briefly describe what his letter to Aunt Alma might say.
3. If Bruce does not "play the game", what might his parents do?

WHAT NOW, SIS?

THINKING ABOUT THE STORY

1. Use one good sentence to describe each of the following people:
   - (a) Johnny
   - (b) Sis
   - (c) Mom
   - (d) Dad
   - (e) Howard

2. Why is Rob important to the story?
3. Find some sentences in the story that show the parents' feelings about people. What are those feelings?
4. Is it possible that Johnny might take Howard home with him for a visit? Why or why not?
5. Might Aunt Alma ("Play the Game") be friendly with this family? Explain.
6. Does the term "playing the game" apply to anyone in this story? Explain.
7. Suggest another title for this story.

THINKING ABOUT THE ENDING

1. Choose one of the following conclusions for the story. Explain your choice.
   (a) Johnny goes to the dean and asks for another roommate.
   (b) The father goes to the dean and demands another roommate for his son.
   (c) Johnny refuses to change roommates.
2. Briefly list two other possible endings.

OUT TO WIN

THINKING ABOUT THE STORY

1. Why do Stewart and Roger want to get Ace out of the game? How do they perform this task?
2. In what ways are Stewart and Roger alike? Different?
3. What do we learn about Stewart's parents? How are they like Johnny's parents ("What Now, Sis?")?
4. **Victory at any cost is the key to success.** How

would Roger and Stewart each feel about
this statement?
5. How are the following stories similar?
   (a) "Walk Proud, Be Proud"
   (b) "Play the Game"
   (c) "What Now, Sis?"
   (d) "Out to Win"
6. Besides the athletes themselves, many other
   people owe their jobs to professional sports.
   What are some careers available to the
   person interested in sports?

THINKING ABOUT THE ENDING

Here are two possible endings: Stewart will
either enter the room or leave the hospital.
1. If Stewart turns around and leaves, can he
   forget what happened? Why or why not?
2. If Stewart goes into the hospital room, what
   might he say to Ace? Plan the conversation
   that Stewart and Ace might have. Write a few
   lines describing their conversation.

MY SISTER, THE $3.00 BILL

THINKING ABOUT THE STORY

1. In what ways is Peggy like a "$3.00 bill"?
2. How does Arnie really feel about his sister?
3. How do you think Peggy's friends really feel
   about her?
4. Does Peggy believe what she says? Why
   does she continue acting in this way?

5. Peggy's father is forced to move to another town or be laid off by his company. Will job security be important to you when you choose a career? Why or why not?

THINKING ABOUT THE ENDING

1. When Peggy sees Tom at the front door, she realizes that she is caught in her own lie. Do you think she will lie again? Why or why not?
2. Write a few sentences in which Peggy successfully gets out of this situation by lying.
3. Write a few sentences which show Peggy admitting her lies to Tom and his reaction.

A WORLD OF HER OWN

THINKING ABOUT THE STORY

1. What kind of world did May want to create for herself? Be specific.
2. Why did she feel it was necessary to create this world?
3. In what ways are May and Peggy ("My Sister, the $3.00 Bill") alike? Different?
4. Whose lies are more serious, May's or Peggy's? Why?
5. May, like Peggy, acts like a "$3.00 bill." How?
6. Peggy, like May, creates a "world of her own." How?
7. May's actions are prompted by a magazine ad. What special skills would you need if you entered the world of advertising or

publishing? Name some job opportunities in these fields.

THINKING ABOUT THE ENDING

1. Does May finally realize that her world is filled with lies? Explain your answer.
2. Will May change her life, or will she go on creating new stories? Defend your answer.
3. If May mails the letter, what effect will this action have on her life?

JUST LIKE YOUR SISTER

THINKING ABOUT THE STORY

1. Why do you think Audrey wants to leave home?
2. Why doesn't the mother want to mention the name "Bernadine"?
3. Bernadine is practically disowned by her mother. Yet her mother seems devoted to prayer and religion. How can you explain this contradiction?
4. Why does Audrey feel so close to Baby?
5. Explain what the mother means by saying the following:
   (a) "The devil finds work for idle hands."
   (b) "Baby's the wage of sin."

THINKING ABOUT THE ENDING

1. Who is at the door?

2. If it is Bernadine coming back home, what will the mother do when she sees her? If it is Martin, will Audrey leave Baby and run away with him?
3. Finish writing the story on your paper.

MY SON, THE DOCTOR

THINKING ABOUT THE STORY

1. Where were Luis and his family born?
2. How would you describe Luis' family? How is your family like this one? How is your family different?
3. Why is Luis so special to his family?
4. Why is the party near the end of the story important to the plot?
5. What reason does Luis give for wanting to join the Peace Corps? What qualities will he need to succeed in this career?
6. "The Sacrifice" might also be a good title for this story. Why?
7. Who would be making a bigger sacrifice, Audrey ("Just Like Your Sister") or Luis?
8. Compare Audrey's mother ("Just Like Your Sister") and Luis' mother.

THINKING ABOUT THE ENDING

1. Why didn't Luis tell his mother earlier what he wanted to do?
2. Will he be able to tell the family what he really plans to do? Why or why not?
3. If Luis decides to stay in school, will he be

satisfied with this decision? Explain your answer.

HONOR THY FATHER AND THY MOTHER

THINKING ABOUT THE STORY

1. What problem do Tony's parents have?
2. What clues are given at the beginning of the story to show that Mr. and Mrs. Stevens have such a problem?
3. At times, Tony had to be both mother and father. Why do Lynn and Willie accept him in this role?
4. How can Mr. Jones change Tony's life?
5. How is Tony's problem similar to that of Audrey ("Just Like Your Sister") and Luis ("My Son, the Doctor")?
6. Who has the hardest decision to make—Audrey, Luis or Tony?

THINKING ABOUT THE ENDING

1. Imagine that Tony decides to leave home. How will his parents manage without him? How will Lynn and Willie get on by themselves?
2. All these questions probably went through Tony's mind when he saw Mr. Jones. Now, try to write an ending for this story. Remember that it will probably be impossible to satisfy all the members of the Stevens family.